THE AMAZING
MRS SHUFFLEWICK

The Life
of Rex Jameson

Third Age Press

ISBN 1 898576 21 1
First edition

Third Age Press Ltd, 2007
Third Age Press, 6 Parkside Gardens
London SW19 5EY
Managing Editor Dianne Norton

Front cover photo from *TV Mirror* 25.06.55 Vol. 4 No. 26
Back cover photo from *A Tribute to Mrs Shufflewick*
Souvenir Programme
Photographs and playbills
from the Patrick Newley collection

Cover & layout design by Dianne Norton
Printed and bound in Great Britain
by Intype Libra London

THE AMAZING MRS SHUFFLEWICK
The Life of of Rex Jameson

by
PATRICK NEWLEY

ABOUT THE AUTHOR

PATRICK NEWLEY is a longstanding contributor to both *The Times* and *The Stage* newspapers. He has also written for *The Daily Express* and many other publications. A frequent broadcaster for the BBC he was press agent for the writers Quentin Crisp and Robin Maugham. He managed the later careers of both the legendary revue artiste Douglas Byng and the comedian Rex Jameson (Mrs Shufflewick).

For Richard Ruck

It's scary up here. So you're scared, you drink and you're not scared. For 50 years I never put a foot on stage without a drink – or any place else come to think of it. (Elaine Stritch)

INTIMATE THEATRE
PALMERS GREEN, N.13
01-886 3798

Commencing Thursday, 6th September, 1973 - At 7.30

FOR 3 NIGHTS ONLY

JOHN FARROW PRESENTS

OLDE TYME MUSIC HALL
WITH

JIMMY WHEELER
RADIO'S STAR COMEDIAN

Miss **BARBARA NEWMAN**
BRITISH, BRIGHT & BREEZY

Mr. **JOHN FARROW**
YOUR WORTHY CHAIRMAN

★ # MRS. SHUFFLEWICK ★

AND FULL STAR BILL

POPULAR PRICES	75p	60p	50p	REDUCTIONS OAP's & PARTIES

BOOK EARLY

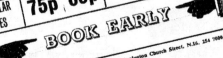

Printed by Beacon Press Ltd. (T.U.), 129 Stoke Newington Church Street, N.16. 254 7004.

Contents

Illustrations

INTRODUCTION

Mrs Shufflewick was a red-nosed, drunken old cockney. She used to prop up the bar in her local ('the Cock and Comfort'), perched precariously on a stool, drinking port and lemon. She had a flowery hat on with a sprig of cherries stuck in it and a battered fur round her neck made of 'genuine untouched pussy'.

'Broadminded to the point of obscenity', she was once married to a pheasant plucker and was formerly known on the variety stage as 'Bubbles Latrine and her educated sheepdogs'.

Mrs S, 'weak willed and easily led', optimistically sought pleasure – 'If I'm not in bed by eleven, I'm going home' she said, but her mind was continually fogged by booze and she invariably ended up stark naked, all but her hairnet, on top of a 29 bus.

Night after night for nearly thirty years Rex Jameson, or 'Shuff' as he was affectionately known, appeared as Mrs

Shufflewick in variety theatres, clubs and on radio and television. He was known as 'the comedian's comedian' and was famed for his immaculate timing and delivery. He wrote nearly all his own material and towards the end of his life became a comic icon. He was respected by the legitimate theatre and made appearances at the Royal Court Theatre in London, Greenwich and The Old Vic. The three live recordings of his act have become collectors items.

But who was Rex Jameson? To his audiences the quiet man behind the outrageous character of Mrs Shufflewick was a mystery. He rarely socialised after a show and would often disappear out of the stage door dressed in an old raincoat, clutching a shopping bag, and disappear into the night.

I knew Rex for 13 years both as his friend and manager. He was a complex, difficult and often brilliantly funny man. Sometimes shy, often obstinate, always exasperating, he could be generous to a tee. Although he was regarded as one of the pioneers of drag he once admitted that he hated the very word: 'I am a comedian in women's clothing,' he said. 'When I first started it wasn't called drag; people were 'dame comedians', people like George Lacey. It wasn't camp at all. It was a man dressed as a woman. I often throw in a line to let an audience know that I'm not all fur and feathers.'

When once asked what the actual skill of drag was he said simply, 'Communication with an audience,' but then added succinctly, 'but if some silly bastard in the government said 'we'll have no more gentlemen dressing up as ladies', I suppose I could get myself a funny suit, a pair of glasses and a funny face and still do the same gags.'

The real thing he had in common with the ribald Mrs Shufflewick was that, like her, he was a notorious drunk. Rex and alcohol seemed to go hand in hand. His favourite drinks were Guinness, often laced with barley wine, or a large Scotch.

Ralph Reader described Rex's act as 'a pocket version of Marie Lloyd', while others compared him to Dan Leno and Arthur Lucan's Old Mother Riley. More accurately some commentators saw elements of the music hall comedienne Nellie Wallace in Mrs Shufflewick and although Mrs S is sexually more advanced than Nellie, they share many points of reference. Both were eccentric and naive, and both elicited sympathy from their audiences. And like Nellie, Mrs S was a whiff of pure music hall. Even her signature tune, borrowed from Marie Lloyd, was *My Old Man Said Follow The Van.*

Rex's relatively short career as a performer — he died at the age of 58 – falls into two distinctive sections. During the first part he was a leading variety performer playing to largely family audiences in theatres and on radio and television. His act was risqué but he was able to adapt or tone it down to suit the various venues. In the second part of his career, when many variety theatres had closed and his heavy drinking made managements wary of booking him, he was 'discovered' by gay audiences in London clubs and pubs and went on to become a cult figure. Ironically, his act as Mrs Shufflewick had changed little and it was not unusual to see him perform a spot on a variety bill one day and then a gay club the next using almost the same material.

He was also lionised in the seventies by comedians such as Barry Cryer, Bob Monkhouse, Barry Humphries and

Roy Hudd — friend and champion of Rex
for many years

Roy Hudd. Hudd described him as 'a comic genius. Even
in his cups Rex was gloriously funny.' Actors too admired
his performances, including Nigel Hawthorne and Simon
Callow. Jonathan Cecil and his wife Anna Sharkey were
self confessed 'Shufflewick groupies'. 'Rex as Mrs Shufflewick was truly one of the great stand-up comics, right
up there with Ken Dodd, Frankie Howerd and even Jack
Benny,' said Jonathan Cecil. Eric Idle was a fan. So was
Bob Hoskins: 'When I was a kid I used to go to the Finsbury
Empire.The funniest act I ever saw was Mrs Shufflewick.
She was brilliant. I had no idea she was a man.'

The Amazing Mrs Shufflewick

As well as alcohol Rex's career was also defined by his homosexuality. Although in the fifties he, like many other gay performers, did not declare his sexuality publicly — his career would have ended if he had — he was for many gay men a link, someone who they could anonymously identify with. When writing this memoir Bryan Hooton wrote to me saying: 'I was born in 1941 so I was a teenager when TV was growing up fast in the 1950s and Rex Jameson as Mrs Shufflewick appeared regularly. I knew that I was gay (although that word had not been invented then) and I thought he must be as well. I loved him.'

It wasn't until the seventies that Rex was openly gay although in his private life he was more apt to be found drinking in a working men's pub in Kentish Town, where he lived, than he was in a glitzy gay bar. He was by nature reserved and conservative and as far removed from the label 'drag queen' as it was possible to be. He read *The Daily Mirror* or *The Sporting Life*, ate meals in greasy spoons, liked betting on the horses and watching 'Carry On' films. He smoked Woodbine cigarettes, wore a flat cap and bought all his clothes in jumble sales. Alcoholic and permanently broke it seems astonishing that he should have become a gay icon.

Showbusiness stories about Rex, particularly those associated with alcohol, are legion. Some of them are true and some are apocryphal. The most famous tale involves Rex arriving at a theatre and being locked into his dressing room by a worried stage manager in an effort to keep him sober. Rex is supposed to have slipped a note under the door, bribing a stagehand to buy him a bottle of whiskey. The stagehand duly feeds the booze via a straw through the keyhole which Rex drinks and thus goes on stage completely smashed. A variation on the story sees him lowering, à la Rapunzel, a string out of the dressing room window to which a stagehand attaches a bottle of booze. Unfortunately, when I asked Rex if the story was true, he denied it.

True or not, few performers ever got themselves into such theatrical scrapes as Rex did and I have included some of the relevant episodes in this memoir.

Rex gave few interviews in his career. However, he did talk in 1972 with the now defunct *Gay News* and in 1980 with BBC producer and writer Michael Pointon. It is from these two interviews together with several private tapes I made with him that all his quotes in this memoir are taken. I have also interspersed selections from his act in italics throughout the book.

Although he was known to many people later in his career as 'Shuff', for the purposes of biography I have used his christian name, Rex, throughout.

PART ONE

Childhood

Few entertainers can have suffered such an identity crisis as Rex Jameson did. Abandoned by his unknown mother at birth, he was brought up by foster parents, christened Rex Coster, and then, after going into showbusiness, changed his surname to Jameson. He created the character of Mrs Shufflewick, a persona so real that theatre managements of the day insisted that he be billed purely as Mrs Shufflewick with no mention of Rex Jameson in the programme.

As Rex's hard-drinking self eventually merged with the equally boozy Mrs Shufflewick he became known simply as 'Shuff'. No one called him Mr Jameson, not even Rex. The original Rex Coster ceased to exist, surfacing only on his death certificate in 1983.

Throughout his career he always remained a private man. Few knew anything of his past, his background, family life or relationships. Most audiences did not even know his real name. Interviews with him were rare and, especially when he had been drinking, he had a habit of distorting his past, often merging fact with fiction. He did not intend to deceive, merely to defend his privacy.

He was born in London on June 11, 1924 and when he was two weeks old his real mother left him on the steps of Trinity College Hospital, Greenwich. He was brought up by foster parents who lived in Southend-on-Sea, a fitting hometown for a comedian whose favourite working venue was always a seaside resort. Southend in the first half of the 20th century was one of the biggest seaside resorts in Britain, with the longest pier — over a mile long — in the country.

It was also the resort most popular with working class Londoners who swarmed to the town in the summer months. They came for the funfairs, winkle stalls, cockles, jellied eels and pubs. There was Kursaal, a giant entertainment complex which had every conceivable amusement for the holidaymaker, Wilby Lunn's concert party on the pier, and variety shows at the Southend Hippodrome.

In the early thirties, when Rex was a boy, stars such as Fred Russell and Harry Champion were regulars at the Hippodrome, and an impoverished and ageing Fred Barnes, the gay music hall singer, could be seen performing in local pubs for small change or a free drink.

When the holidaymakers were not there Southend retained a glimmer of the faded elegance of the select watering place to which 'Prinny', the Prince Regent, relegated his Princess Caroline to stay in what is now Royal Terrace.

In Rex's stage act Mrs Shufflewick is a born and bred, genteel, working class cockney who lives in the East End. Rex's upbringing could not have been more different. His foster parents, George and Mabel Coster, lived from 1924 to 1930 at 24 Westcliff Parade, a magnificent three-storey early Victorian house on the clifftop with views straight across the Thames estuary and an ornate bandstand within earshot.

From 1931 to 1937, they were at the somewhat less grand 5 Whitefriars Crescent, two storeys high and a short distance away from the clifftop.

Rex's childhood in Southend was a solitary and uneventful one. Slightly built, almost puny, he had a mop of wavy ginger hair. Although never shy, he was reserved and spent much of his time on his own listening to the radio or going to the cinema. In later years he recalled his love of radio shows such as *Bandwaggon* with Arthur Askey and Richard 'Stinker' Murdoch and *ITMA* with Tommy Handley which he would listen to on a crystal set.

In Southend's long defunct cinemas, such as The Mascot and The Rivoli, he saw anarchic early Marx Brothers films, Will Hay, W C Fields, Lubitsch and Capra comedies as well as nailbiting weekly serials such as *Flash Gordon Returns to Mars*.

'When I was very young there used to be sophisticated Hollywood films with people like Adolphe Menjou,' he said. 'They were lovely, you could enjoy yourself.'

He always referred to his foster parents as Uncle George and Auntie Mabel and had a special affinity with the latter. 'Auntie Mabel was a wonderful person,' he said. 'She had a thing about cats. But I was terrified of Uncle George. He used to kick all the cats out of the back door and she'd let them in round the front. She used to have a lady friend and they would go out together to the pub on Sunday mornings.'

An element of the bizarre — something that Rex was to become almost synonymous with in later life — made an early appearance in his childhood. 'Auntie Mabel used to put a bottle of bleach and a bottle of cider down by the side of the stove,' he said. 'So when she and her friend came back from the pubs after they had shut they would have a little drop to keep them going. One day her friend picked up the bleach instead of the cider. She was dead in about ten minutes.'

Rex was educated locally but in 1938 the family moved from Southend to Alsen Road in Holloway in North London. George and Mabel would have been aware of war impending but they could not have chosen a worse area in London to live. Because of the importance of shunting yards at nearby Finsbury Park, an anti-aircraft battery was stationed there, and a barrage balloon at Highbury Fields. Despite these defences (or because of them) Highbury attracted the attention of the enemy, not only with conventional bombs, but also with sticks of fire-bombs, V1s, V11s and land mines, so that even those buildings that were not destroyed, lost ceilings and glass.

For Rex, a quiet teenager who had grown up with all the childish delights of the seaside, living in London during the war, and particularly the Blitz of 1940, must have been harrowing. The anti-aircraft barrage, wrote J B Priestley, made a sound 'as if gigantic doors were being slammed to' in the sky, while the sound of distant bombs was a 'crump' that shook the ground. The commotion made by the mere passage of a bomb through the air was astonishing. Whole houses shook, objects rattled on kitchen tables. People hated the sound of the sirens. 'Banshee howlings,' Churchill called them. 'As if the darkened countryside, like a vast trapped animal, were screaming at us,' said Priestley.

London air raid shelters varied. Some were communal like those underground at Islington Green, Finsbury Square, and on the platforms of Underground stations. Also underground were the Anderson shelters of corrugated iron installed in private gardens, but the most popular in Holloway and Islington were the windowless brick huts constructed in the street for general use.

The bombing of London was repeated for 76 nights on end but the men, women and children who suffered the Blitz discovered a new solidarity absent during the war until then. The cheerfulness of the Blitz was certainly not a myth and those who stayed in London had reason to be proud.

Rex's home town fared no better. In common with many other coastal towns in the south east, Southend suffered frequent hit and run attacks from enemy aircraft. Many shops were closed and boarded up, and there was much evidence of bomb damage. The pier had been taken over by the navy, and had become HMS Leigh. The Kursaal amusement park was shut and the seafront quiet and desolate.

All road signposts to the town were removed. Checkpoints manned by military and civil police were set up on all roads leading in to the town. Southend became virtually inaccessible to outsiders.

At the beginning of the war Rex often took refuge in the cinema, sometimes going on his own or with Richard, John and Mary Hinde, three young neighbours of his in Alsen Road. Many cinemas were kept open in air raids, some of them offering a night's shelter, with entertainment thrown in. When the last advertised showing ended, if bombs were falling outside, the full programme would be repeated, plus three stand-by feature films, interludes on the organ, a sing-song and an amateur talent show. Rex remembered one record breaking programme lasting for eight hours after normal closing time, with the audience sleeping beneath the circle for shelter.

A number of theatres remained open, notably the Finsbury Park Empire, a beautiful Frank Matcham designed building on the corner of St Thomas and Prah Road. Although Rex had no ambitions to become a performer, it was at the Finsbury Park Empire that he got his first taste for showbusiness.

'When I was fourteen I went to the Empire every Monday night,' he said. 'I paid 6d in the gallery. That really put me on the road to showbusiness because I saw all the stars there. They really were stars in those days. I loved the whole atmosphere of it. Later I had the wonderful pleasure of working with some of the people I saw at the Finsbury Park Empire, people like Jimmy James who to my mind was the most wonderful comedian. And I saw people like Gracie Fields. It was magic.'

Being brought up in a seaside resort he had acquired a sweet tooth — a taste for two penny bars of chocolate and seaside rock — so wartime food rationing came as a shock. By early 1941 when merchant ships were being sunk at the rate of three a day, shortages were at their worst. Such items as meat, butter, margarine, bacon, and tea were rationed by weight. Two of the most disliked wartime institutions, dried egg and dried milk, were brought in from the United States. The shortage of sugar led to a desperate search for sweetness. 'Raw carrots added to steamed puddings and cakes will sweeten them,' promised the Ministry of Food.

Everyone, whatever their age, was involved in war work of some kind, even if it was only Digging for Victory, by growing vegetables in a garden or an allotment, or giving their aluminium cooking pots to be recycled as aircraft parts. Those under 18 were recruited to organisations such as the scouts or training groups run by the services. Rex joined a training group learning first aid and helping the civil defence as a messenger.

The Gang Show

Rex received his call-up papers in 1942 and went into the RAF. 'I was stationed at Boscombe Down for about eighteen months,' he said. 'We had one of Ralph Reader's *Gang Shows* come to our station and I was on the back-stage staff. One of the fellas said, 'Why don't you apply to the Air Ministry for a posting to the Gang Show — it saves carrying a gun about all bleedin' day.' And that's what I did. I went up to London and had an audition with Ralph Reader and was taken on.'

Ralph Reader's name is synonymous with the boy scout *Gang Shows* but before the war he was a leading choreographer and producer both on Broadway, where he worked with Al Jolson, and in the West End. When war was declared Reader was commissioned into the RAF as an intelligence officer. As a cover for his activities 12 members of his pre-war scout *Gang Show* were formed into the first *RAF Gang Show*. The Air Ministry recognised that such shows would make perfect cover for Reader's activities.

Ralph Reader, creator of the *Gang Shows*. He described
Rex's act as *'a pocket version of Marie Lloyd'*

Rex was posted to Cairo where he became a member of
the No. 4 Gang Show Unit which travelled around North
Africa, Italy and Cyprus. There were about a dozen men
in each of Reader's show and they did everything from
appearing in corny comedy sketches to singing sentimental songs and building makeshift stages. Their working
conditions were sparse and often hazardous. One day they
might be entertaining in a NAFFI canteen and the next on
the back of a lorry in the desert. Wind often stirred up the
sand which surged across the desert in a blinding storm.
Sand stung the men's' faces, hands and knees, crept into
the nostrils, grinding between their teeth. It would spread
a gritty powder over food and drink, would mat hair, line

clothes and stick to the warmest parts of the men's' bodies. But no matter where a unit was, Reader insisted on full make-up, full costume, one hundred per cent effort, and the Gang Show backcloth, a light blue curtain with the embroidered words '*Gang Show*'.

**On tour, entertaining the troops in North Africa in 1946.
Rex is at the back of the bus peering out of the window**

The list of comedians who rose from the RAF Gang Show is an oddly mixed bag of British comedy: Peter Sellers, Graham Stark, Cardew Robinson, Reg 'Confidentially' Dixon, Billy Wells, The Cox Twins and many more.

A flight sergeant was in charge of each unit but the rest were airmen. Rex's flight sergeant was Tony Hancock. 'When we were in Cairo and we had time off, Tony and I would head for the nearest bars and drink ourselves stupid all day,' said Rex. 'There wasn't much beer so we drank Scotch. All the other men went to the brothels but that wasn't for me.'

If the war gave Rex his first taste of hard liquor then it also gave him his first opportunity to appear in female costume and, with his slim figure, ginger hair and pale looks, he was often cast as the leading lady in comedy sketches. A 1943 photograph shows him in a cascading blonde wig and shiny evening gown playing the Princess in a *Gang Show* skit of *Jack and the Beanstalk* opposite airman Wally Sheppard's Jack. In later years Sheppard described the skit as 'pure *It 'Aint Half Hot Mum*', a reference to the seventies TV comedy series. Rex also appeared in sketches as a comic vicar — a routine that he was to develop when he turned professional.

Many of the performers who appeared in the RAF all-male *Gang Shows* showed a remarkable flair for female impersonation, most outstanding of these (apart from Rex) being Billy Wells who began his stage career in 1928 but turned to drag when he took part in the *RAF Gang Shows.*

Peace broke up the *RAF Gang Shows* but Rex was to remain a lifelong friend of both Tony Hancock and Ralph Reader. As a comedian in his own

Rex as the Princess and Wally Sheppard as Jack in an *RAF Gang Show* **skit of** *Jack and the Beanstalk*

The Amazing Mrs Shufflewick

right Rex had an all too intuitive understanding of Hancock's personal and professional insecurities. Ironic then, that Reader, who had known these two unique comic talents from the start of their careers, should comment in 1974 that 'had circumstances been different, Rex would have been as big a star (in an entirely different way) as Tony Hancock'.

Rex was demobbed on November 6, 1946 and given a grey chalk-striped demob suit (possibly the smartest piece of clothing he was ever to wear) and £60 gratuity. '*The Gang Show* gave me the taste for showbiz,' he said. 'I thought this is marvellous, this life, getting pissed all the time, not having to work in the morning, so I turned professional. There was a broadcaster called Sam Costa popular at the time so I had to change my name. I took the name Jameson after the whiskey.'

Happy Hour

Rex got his first showbiz break when he auditioned, and subsequently became, one of Bryan Michie's 'Discoveries'. Michie, a burly, outsize figure usually seen wearing a dress suit, became famous as a talent scout in post-war years, a sort of precursor to TV's Hughie Green, he was noted for discovering the young Ernie Wise. He produced several touring stage shows which featured his discoveries and in 1947 Rex appeared in *The Bryan Michie Happy Hour Show* which toured Granada cinemas around the country.

Michie compered the show and Rex appeared both as a comic vicar and, in a new creation, a then unnamed cockney charlady. Prominent also in the cast was a young impressionist, Johnny Hamp, who later became a talent scout himself and, in the seventies, the successful producer of ITV's *The Comedians*.

The Bryan Michie Happy Hour Show toured for two years. Michie was impressed with Rex's talent and in 1949 persuaded him to audition for light entertainment radio producer Bryan Sears at the BBC. It was a timely audition that accidentally led to the birth of Mrs Shufflewick.

The Bryan Michie Happy Hour Show Granada Theatres Tour 1949/50. Shuff is 3rd from right back row

'I went to the BBC and was put in this room with a great microphone,' said Rex. 'In those days the sound booths looked like a padded cell with mattresses for walls. Somebody said, 'You can begin now,' so I did my comedy vicar act, 'Ah good evening to you my flock, and now you can flock off . . .' and before I could say anything more they said, 'Stop, stop, we don't want this!' In those days you couldn't do any jokes about religion. There was the censor.

The Amazing Mrs Shufflewick

So Bryan Sears asked me if I could do anything else and I said I could do a charlady act. He told me to come back in a week and think of a name for the character. I went home and wrote this routine and after a few glasses of whiskey I came up with names like Mrs Brandyshuttle, Ethel La Plunge and Mrs Shufflewick. Bryan picked Mrs Shufflewick and that's how the act started. I went on to *Variety Bandbox* (on 4 May 1950) and then got other radio shows like *London Lights, Midday Music Hall* and so on.'

Rex was not the very first female impersonator to appear on radio. That honour went to the revue and panto Dame star Douglas Byng who sang some of his own risqué songs on air in the 1930s but Rex was the first artiste to actually perform in female attire in BBC studios when radio shows were broadcast live.

The Birth of Mrs Shufflewick

Hello dears, Mrs Shufflewick is the name. Me measurements are thirty-eight, thirty-eight wiv me shoes on. Here we all are then, full of port and ready to sport, and full of gin and ready for . . .

The original Mrs Shufflewick (her christian name was Gladys) was a slightly refined cockney char with a high pitched voice and a penchant for drink. 'Weak willed and easily led', she had an unnamed husband and a close friend Lily, with whom she often went on disastrous holidays — usually in Blackpool — or mammoth pub crawls.

My friend Lil and I decided to go to the seafront and seventeen pubs later we got there. It was

*worth it because I had a plate of whelks and Lily
had a plate of cockles. And then I had a meat pie,
oh, and then we half a stick of rock each, and then
we had some cider — and a crab sandwich. And
some candyfloss. And do you know I think it was
that meat pie that upset me. Then we moved next
door for a pint and we stayed till ten past gone.
And do you know when we left Lil was so drunk I
could hardly see her.*

Rex claimed that Mrs Shufflewick was based on his foster mother, 'Auntie' Mabel, though it is highly unlikely that Mrs Coster's drinking habits were in the same league as the inebriate Mrs S. 'My auntie Mabel was more like Mrs Shufflewick than I am,' he said. 'She had a funny way of walking, you'd think she was on her way to the toilet. But she was a wonderful person and I think I really based my act on her.'

Rex's rise to fame in the world of post war light entertainment was a relatively swift one. His act was something of a novelty and he had few rivals. For his radio broadcasts he was often billed simply as Mrs Shufflewick rather than Rex Jameson and many people believed that Mrs S was a real person.

'The utter believability of Rex's Mrs Shufflewick was something that astounded me from the start,' said fellow radio star impressionist Peter Goodwright. 'On the broadcasts, her adventures with people she met were always hilarious but I was more intrigued by the inevitability of disaster which underlined the stories — and which, seemingly, Mrs S accepted as the norm. The audiences used to love him, and I realise (with hindsight) how very well disciplined he was with his material for these broadcasts — rarely going beyond the stricter rules which governed things 'rude' existing at the time.'

Last night — I must tell you this — I was sitting up in bed at about half past seven, mending a puncture. I had a blow-out. I was sticking this patch on when all of a sudden I had it coming on again. You know, one of me hot flushes. Do you get them ? Oooh, I do. I have to blow down me blouse on the buses. I thought it's no good me sitting here sweating, so I thought the best thing is to slip into something loose and pop down to the local for a drop of you know. . .

Live shows such as *Midday Music Hall* and *Variety Bandbox* were usually broadcast from the BBC's Paris Studios in Lower Regent Street or the Playhouse Theatre in Northumberland Avenue and Rex always arrived in full costume, playing the part of Mrs S to the hilt. 'He would arrive in drag in a taxi,' said Peter Goodwright. 'I have a vivid recollection of a cab drawing up beside me in Lower Regent Street, Rex creeping out, and paying the driver from a little purse which appeared from his handbag, in what appeared to be very small change — chatting the while and finishing with, 'Well, there you are dear, — and there's a shilling for yourself. Don't spend it all at once'.'

The huge popularity of fifties radio stars such as Rex led to audiences demanding to see their favourite performers in stage shows and Rex was signed up by Joe Collins (father of Jackie and Joan), then one of the most powerful variety agents of the day. Collins' clients in the fifties included Hal Monty, Diana Dors, Dennis Spicer and a young Larry

Grayson, to name but a few. Rex's variety dates for Collins ranged from touring with the volatile singer Dorothy Squires (with whom he was to be reunited at the London Palladium in the seventies) to appearing in West End night clubs such as The Astor and The Embassy.

'In the early days I used to work a bit like Nellie Wallace with a feather boa,' said Rex. 'Then one day I was doing a variety bill with Betty Driver, who went on to be a star in *Coronation Street*, and she said 'Why don't you smarten Mrs S up and dress rather 'nicely' but still keep the same character?' Which I did and I found it worked.'

Mrs S was outwardly prim in the fifties and her tales saucy rather than lewd but no matter what the denouement she would invariably end with a sentimental monologue, half spoken, half sung:

> *I'm just a simple mother*
> *And it's hard to realise*
> *My kids have all grown up and gone away.*
> *I often think about them*
> *In the days when they were young*
> *I've watched them in their work and in their play.*
> *I'm just a simple mother*
> *And I worry night and day*
> *And I think about them everywhere they go*
> *And though it may seem strange*
> *I know I'll never change*
> *And not one of them would want me to — I know.*

In 1953 he made a rare excursion into legit theatre, billed as Rex Jameson at the Coliseum Theatre Harrow, in a series of light plays including *Smiling Through* and the unbelievably titled *Story of the Rosary* ('suggested', it

Rex appearing in a rare legitimate role at the Coliseum
Theatre, Harrow, in 1953

boldly said on the posters, by 'the world famous song'). 'I was in a show at Blackpool and I had a telegram to go and see Alfred Denville who ran the Coliseum,' said Rex. 'So I went to see him and he said in this actor laddie voice 'Ah, I'd like you to appeah in my plaihs,' and I said 'I'm not an actor,' and he said 'I've heard about you and that your timing is good' and all this balls. Then suddenly a script arrived and we did four different plays and I hated every minute of it. Straight plays with no comedy in them. I was drunk for most of the run.'

The Windmill

Drunk or not Rex's name had come to the attention of Vivian Van Damm who ran London's Windmill Theatre, famous for its non-stop variety, tableaux of scantily clad girls and audiences who were often made up of men in raincoats. The tiny, but always packed, theatre in Great Windmill Street, Soho, had flourished during the war under its famous slogan 'We never closed' (once interpreted by a showgirl with a lisp as 'we never clothed') because all the girls had never stopped dancing while bombs were falling around. It had become a beacon for millions of servicemen on their way to or on the way back from war. Many unknown comics had made their name such as Bruce Forsyth, Peter Sellers, Harry Secombe and Jimmy Edwards and the formidable Van Damm (or VD as he was cynically known) asked Rex to audition for a possible season.

'I was terribly nervous standing there in front of him,' said Rex. 'The Windmill rehearsal room was like a dead garage. But for some reason he liked my act and he gave me a six month contract. As I was leaving, he said 'It's a lovely act, Rex, but you must get yourself some double entendres'. I hadn't a clue what he meant. I thought he wanted me to get something to stick on my costume. I was really in a daze because in those days the Windmill was almost like the London Palladium. I ended up there for three years. You did the same act six shows a day; you did it every hour. For the first three shows you had men in raincoats playing with their tortoises and then you got a normal audience for the last two shows at night. It was a good, but bloody hard, training ground.'

Tony Hancock, who appeared at the Windmill in 1948 as part of the double act Hancock and (Derek) Scott, recalled that the 2.00pm show was the worst. 'If they didn't like you in the first show, they positively hated you in the second,' he said. 'It taught me to die bravely. At 3.30pm things were better as the pubs had closed and audiences were more relaxed.'

Hancock's insecurity was often noted by Rex: 'In the fifties I was appearing at the Astor Club in cabaret and Tony was topping the bill at a theatre round the corner. I once caught his act from the side of the stage and he went down a bomb. The audience adored him. But he came off stage shaking. He looked at me and said, 'I've been a failure, Rex — it's all a disaster'.

Rex was one of the most successful acts to play the Windmill — he was paid £50 per week – and remained a personal favourite of Van Damm. He was also admired by his fellow performers: 'I remember playing the Windmill in one of the seasons Rex did there and his delivery and timing were superb,' said Bill Pertwee, another comic who got his early break at the theatre.

Tony Hancock, drinking pal and Rex's Flight Sergeant in
the RAF Gang Shows in North Africa

In between shows at the Windmill, and wearing his customary full drag, Rex would frequent the Bear and Staff pub in Charing Cross Road, then a popular haunt for theatricals and gay men. It was something of a discreet refuge in a time when homosexuality was not only against the law, but also actively persecuted by the police. Homosexual acts carried a sentence of seven years imprisonment. The notoriously reactionary Home Secretary, Sir David Maxwell Fyffe, was convinced that homosexuality threatened the British way of life and he and his colleagues believed that they had a mission to liberate British society from this 'evil'. The popular press fuelled the flames of fear and suspicion with articles on such topics as '*How to Spot a Homo*' (sports jackets and suede shoes) and a feature in the *Sunday Pictorial* called '*Evil Men*' observed: 'Homosexuality is rife in the theatrical profession . . . they have mincing ways . . . call each other girls' names openly . . . wear women's clothes.'

In 1953 the actor Sir John Gielgud was convicted of importuning a male person and fined ten pounds. At the time he was appearing in the West End with Dame Sybil Thorndike in *A Day at the Sea*. After he had paid the fine, he went to the Adelphi Theatre for the evening show. Dame Sybil said to the rest of the cast: 'Here comes John. Remember, it could happen to you, it could happen to me.'

One of Rex's drinking pals in the Bear and Staff was a young Danny Carroll, an ex-merchant navy seaman turned drag artiste, who was appearing in a drag revue entitled *Men Only* at the nearby Irving Theatre Club. He went on to become world famous as the rib-nudging, hip-shaking and wildly glamorous Danny La Rue. Rex and Danny's friendship was a special one which lasted over thirty years

**Danny La Rue — who first met Rex in the late 1940s
and remained a loyal friend for life**

and although Danny's fortunes rose and Rex's declined the bond between the two performers — one of great respect and affection — always remained the same.

I was standing at the bar, minding my own business, and all of a sudden the door opened, and this sailor walked in. I think he must have been in the Navy meself because he kissed me on both cheeks. And I was doing me shoelaces up at the time. He turned to me and he said, 'Would you care for a little something between your lips?' I said 'What did you have in mind?' He said 'Oh, just a little something to shove down your guts.' I said 'Well, that's very kind of you, I'm rather partial to a large port.' So he went off and he came back later with a picture of Southampton Docks.'

Rex once told me that he had had a close affair with a woman shortly after the war but it had not lasted. He never revealed the woman's name. Throughout his life he enjoyed the company of women but was sexually more attracted to men and was not averse to chatting up men in a bar or theatrical club. He also went 'cottaging', importuning men in public conveniences. The most famous 'cottage' in the forties and fifties was in Dansey Place, near Shaftesbury Avenue. During World War Two it became a favourite haunt of American servicemen, much to the gratification of regular cottagers.

Not every one of Rex's sexual encounters was successful. Circus showman Gerry Cottle — heterosexual and teetotal — recalled that as a naive young man he was taken to the Bear and Staff pub by boisterous friends and found himself in the gents being propositioned by a drunken Mrs Shufflewick (wearing her trademark pearl-drop earrings, damson velvet coat, and parched salad of a hat) whom he took to be an elderly Soho transvestite. 'The rogue stood next to me in the urinal and made a very definite physical pass at me,' he said. 'Get your hands off me or I'll swear I'll knock your block off!' I yelped and rushed out of the pub in all of a fluster.'

Little is known of Rex's gay relationships in the fifties but writer Hugh Small recalled an intriguing friendship: 'In 1954, when I was 11, I went to live in a house in Harley Street. The previous occupant left behind a butler, whom I only knew as Wilkinson. He was a kindly, baby-faced man who took a great liking to me and used to invite me down to his basement rooms to show me his treasures and to talk about life's disappointments. Wilkinson's best friend was Rex Jameson, who often came to our house to visit him. They also frequented the Dover Castle pub around the corner which was a hangout for BBC types. I often dreamed that he might have taken care of Rex in their declining years.' Sadly no further knowledge has been gleaned of the kindly Wilkinson although there is something surreal in the thought that the character of Mrs S might have ended up with her own butler.

The most off-beat relationship that Rex enjoyed must surely have been his long standing friendship with Hylda Baker, the Bolton born comedienne famed for her catchphrase 'She knows y'know!' and who, onstage, looked remarkably like Mrs Shufflewick herself. A tiny, forceful figure, she spewed malapropisms like machine gunfire and fought her way in the male dominated world of variety to become one of its biggest stars. She was also infamous for her explosive

temperament and drove people mad in the theatre by insisting that her pet monkeys went everywhere with her. In the sixties and seventies her trademark jerky mannerisms and flair for the double entendre made her a huge name on TV in shows such as *Nearest and Dearest* and *Not On Your Nellie.*

Comedienne Hylda Baker who once proposed mariage to Rex

Like Rex, Hylda was insecure. She and Rex had met in variety in the early fifties and found a mutual rapport with each other. They shared the same quirky sense of humour and Rex would often visit her at her flat in Torrington Place, round the corner from the British Museum. 'There were monkeys all over the place,' he said. 'I liked Hylda very much. She once asked me to marry her but I said no. I couldn't have gone through with it. It would have been unfair to her.'

Television

Rex's stock as a comic was riding high in 1955 when in January he was reunited with his mentor Ralph Reader for a TV series *It's a Great Life*, which also starred Terry Scott, and the same year he was voted TV Personality of the Year by the *TV Mirror* who put a colour picture of Mrs S on their front cover. A spoof article, not written by Rex, in the same issue was called '*Mrs Shufflewick — My Romantic Day*'.

In March 1955 agent Joe Collins took the front page of *The Performer*, the precursor of *The Stage Newspaper*, to advertise a new BBC Radio series, *Pertwee's Progress*, which Rex was to co-star with Jon Pertwee. Although the series was a success, Rex and Pertwee did not get on together. 'Pertwee was difficult to work with, especially in rehearsals,' said Rex. 'To put it mildly, he was a cunt.'

The following year he starred at the Winter Gardens in Blackpool with Dave King and Shani Wallis and he enjoyed further TV success when he was paired with the great northern comedian Norman Evans in *The Norman Evans Show* which ran from April to June. Evans was a brash and immensely likeable performer who often worked in drag and was noted for his *Over the Garden Wall* routine playing Fanny Fairbottom, a mob-capped, ample-bosomed harridan, hanging out her washing: 'What did you say? That woman at number seven? Is she? Gerraway! Well, I'm not surprised. No, really. She's asked for it. I knew what she was as soon as I saw her! And that coalman, I wouldn't put it past him, either . . . Not since he shouted 'Whoa' to his horse from her bedroom window!'

'Norman was a wonderful person,' said Rex. 'He was so easy going and a brilliant comedian. You would have thought that the two of us clashed — two drag characters — but he was unique and no one else could do his routines. We got on very well together. It was northern and southern comedy on TV and it just merged.'

As a variety comic Rex was well aware of the differences in regional humour. In between television and radio shows Joe Collins had booked him on a punishing tour of regional variety theatres. 'I worked every bloody week of the year,' said Rex. 'I had to go down on my knees to get a week

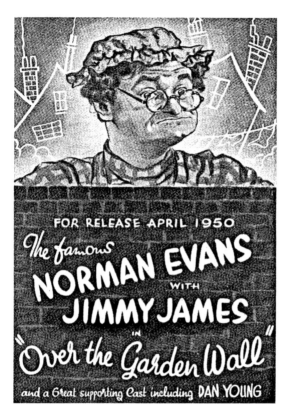

FOR RELEASE APRIL 1950

The famous

NORMAN EVANS

WITH

JIMMY JAMES

IN

"Over the Garden Wall"

and a Great supporting Cast including DAN YOUNG

North country dame comedian Norman Evans who co-starred with Rex in TV shows in the 1950s

off. I had this contract which was 42 weeks of the year guaranteed money, but Joe Collins saw bloody well that I worked 52.'

He worked as far north as Scotland but was happiest working in the south: 'London is the best place for me because Mrs S is basically a cockney character,' he said. 'Lancashire's very difficult, I don't think they like southern comics. I did a week at the Wigan Hippodrome, top of the bill — I had just done six weeks at the Coventry Hippodrome with The Goons — absolute joy, because the audiences were marvellous and you had nothing to worry about. When I went to Wigan and I opened my mouth I did not get a titter from Monday to Saturday. It's hard work up north, Sheffield, Doncaster and up that way. You've really got to get your knickers in a twist to get a laugh. They're more critical in the north than in the south.'

However, when once asked whether he would inject local humour into his act his answer was emphatically no: 'It's fatal to do that because audiences know jolly well you're not northern. If you start doing that they get a bit antagonistic about it.'

I'm always glad to get back to London because, you know
I'm a cockney bred and born,
and there's one place that I love,
that calls me back wherever I may roam,
with its bobbies and its barrows
and its little cocky sparrows,
this place to me is always home sweet home.
Good old Saturday night up West,
where there's everything that's best
and lights shine like stars way up in heaven.
But my heart it starts to beat
when I'm walking down the street
'cos they close up all the pubs dead on eleven!

Away from the theatre Rex spent most of his time either in betting shops of going to his beloved cinemas. He saw few theatre shows, having little interest in legit theatre but occasionally dropped in to a stage door to say hello to variety pals such as Frankie Howerd, who was to remain his favourite comedian. *Look Back in Anger* passed him by, as did Wesker, Pinter and the whole of the kitchen sink shazaam. He was happier sitting in darkened Odeon or Gaumont cinemas, puffing on a Woodbine, in the company of the early 'Carry On' or 'Doctor' films.

In many ways he was fortunate to become a star in the last days of variety. He topped bills, often over then up and coming performers such as Morecambe and Wise and Frankie Howerd, and was around to meet many of his variety idols such as Max Miller and Nellie Wallace. By the end of the fifties, variety, as he knew it, was on its last legs and many of the theatres were making way for bingo halls or demolition. 'I was lucky to be around then', he said. 'I had the last ten years of variety. My timing was only learnt from working in all those theatres.'

Like most touring variety pros he stayed in theatrical digs, experiences of which have provided most actors with a lifetime of anecdotes about oversexed landladies or atrocious cooking. Some digs were notorious, others hospitable. There were some so good that artistes appearing on spring or autumn tours didn't even have to write and say they were coming. The landladies, when they saw the bills of the various shows, knew which artistes would be staying with them and prepared accordingly.

'I remember staying in one digs and in the morning, when I came down to breakfast, there was my bacon and eggs on the table, moving,' recalled Rex. 'Moving on the plate — floating in fat. I sat down and the landlady stood in front of the fire with a fag in her mouth and her eyes screwed up. She said 'Did yer hear us laffing last night?' 'No,' I said. 'I was tired, I went straight off to sleep.' 'Laffing fit to bust we were.' 'Oh really?' 'Our bitch is on heat, you see, and we had the dog in to her — right on the table where you're sitting now!'

I went to Blackpool for the weekend. Oooh, my
feet. I was glad when I got to that boarding

house. What a place though! It looked alright from the outside you know, the bay windows and ivy creeping round the door. Never sober that woman, Ivy — and she was the landlady. She said 'Come along, I'll take you up to the Tudor room. It was too. Her Alsation had chewed the curtains, chewed the carpet and chewed the bedspread. She said 'What would you like for breakfast?' I said 'I'd like some toast when you're ready', so she brought me half a loaf, a box of matches and a blow lamp.'

The decline of variety also coincided with changes in light entertainment on the radio. 'In the fifties I used to do a lot of radio,' said Rex. 'About ten different shows a year. Then they stopped it all and put on record shows so they wouldn't have to pay large fees to performers. I regret the passing of radio variety. You got a lot more back from that audience than you did on television. I think a television audience is sort of ready made. They'll laugh at anything, whereas in a radio show you've got to work bloody hard to get laughs.'

Changes or not Rex still commanded star billing. In just ten years since making his debut in the RAF Gang Shows, he had created the character of Mrs Shufflewick, topped bills in theatre and radio, scripted much of his own material, appeared in legit theatre and won several awards. But his drinking habits had got worse, much of his income had gone on gambling and by 1960 he was declared bankrupt.

The Slippery Slope

Do you like this fur, girls ? It cost two hundred pounds. I didn't pay for it meself; I met two hundred fellas with a pound each. So I was alright — I wasn't done, was I? I can't remember meself now; it's the gin and tonic, it fogs the brain. This is very rare you know, this fur. This is known in the trade as 'untouched pussy' — which as you know is unobtainable in the West End of London at the moment. And I don't think there's much knocking around here tonight . . .

The beginning of the sixties proved to be an unexpected boom in his career. Mrs S swung with the times and although she never wore a mini-skirt, dropped acid or danced to the Beatles, she never stopped working. During that decade, long before the advent of cheap air travel and budget foreign holidays, seaside summer shows reigned supreme in Britain. The social revolution and the coming of the railways in the 19th century opened up the prospect of seaside holidays and enjoyment for the masses, and by the sixties there were over 300 annual summer shows on offer through the country. A glance through any of the summer show editions of *The Stage* newspaper of the period show that resorts such as Blackpool and Great Yarmouth boasted up to half a dozen shows each, all of them featuring variety names from radio and television.

In 1962 Rex co-starred with the irascible TV quizmaster Hughie Green (revealed after his death to be the father of troubled TV presenter Paula Yates) and Irish singer Ruby Murray at the Winter Gardens in Margate in *The Hughie Green Spectacular* and he went on during the decade to guest star in summer shows in Blackpool, Great Yarmouth, Jersey, and Broadstairs. His spot in such shows usually ran to twelve minutes, sometimes twice nightly, and he often appeared in sketches as well. He earned good money but much of it now went on paying back taxes and the rest on drink or gambling. With Rex, booze and betting went hand in hand.

Aren't the price of things dreadful these days ? I went out shopping this morning. I bought half a pound of Summer County margarine, a packet of ginger biscuits and four bottles of gin — and do you know it came to nearly twenty-four quid ? I shall have to give up those ginger biscuits . . .

The closing of the Metropolitan Theatre — known all over the world as 'the Met' — on Good Friday, 12 April 1963, must have been a poignant moment in British theatre history, a sounding death knell for the great days of variety. At the closing performance Rex was part of a star packed bill which included genuine music hall greats such as Hetty King and Ida Barr, as well as variety stalwarts Tommy Trinder, Issy

METROPOLITAN THEATRE
EDGWARE ROAD, W.2   phone AMB 2478

ALL STAR CHARITY SHOW
in aid of the
VARIETY ARTISTES' BENEVOLENT FUND

GOOD **FRIDAY APRIL 12 at 7.30** p.m.

THE FOLLOWING ARTISTES HAVE DEFINITELY PROMISED TO APPEAR ENGAGEMENTS PERMITTING

ISSY BONN	WYN CALVIN
CHRISTINE CAMPBELL	JIMMY FRENCH
HETTY KING	JOHNNY LOCKWOOD
TREVOR MORETON	TED RAY
EDDIE REINDEER	JEAN SCOTT
MRS. SHUFFLEWICK	SIRDANI
THE SQUARE PEGS	TOMMY TRINDER
DICKIE VALENTINE	ERIC WATTS & PAULINE TERRI

IVAN DOZIN & his Orchestra
and many other famous stars of stage and television

LONDON'S MOST FAMOUS MUSIC HALL
BOOK NOW 7'6 10'- 12'6 15'- Licensed Bar

Bonn, Dickie Valentine, Ted Ray and Wyn Calvin. The theatre was held in affection by many and was memorably captured on film in the 1949 police drama *The Blue Lamp* in which an ebullient 'Two Ton' Tessie O'Shea can be seen on stage belting out a number while playing the ukelele.

The Met's closing night was a night of memories and fond regret and hundreds of people had to be turned away. Victor Wilson, the general manager, put it succinctly at the beginning of the evening: 'Everyone wants to come on a night like this. If they had been years ago, we wouldn't be closing tonight.' The Met was eventually demolished to make way for the ugly Marylebone flyover and on its original site now stands the imposing and bleak top security Paddington Green Police Station.

Throughout the sixties Mrs S herself had become decidedly less genteel, less innocent and began to get more boozy. She swore occasionally, frequently had one glass too many and was often thrown out of her local pub altogether. In real life Rex began to acquire a reputation as a lush and stories about his off-beat and drunken behaviour, both onstage and off, were legion in showbusiness.

Bob Monkhouse worked with Rex on an up-market charity ball in the early sixties. 'Shuff was marvellous with posh audiences,' he said. 'When cabaret time came I went on to introduce the acts and struggled to get polite laughter for five minutes. But then out shuffled Shuff and the difficult gathering became a pushover. One sniffy, disapproving gaze from that cartoon hag brought the first gale of laughter. Shuff hitched her shawl, poked at her pathetic hat and used the simplest jokes in her repertoire to convulse them. With eyes occasionally glazing over and a tottering stance, it seemed a brilliant, funny and accurate portrayal of an old biddy who's guzzled enough alcohol to strip the paint off the QE2 — which, of course, Shuff had. He was just a gnat's breath the right side of being incapable.

After the cabaret and deeply inebriated, he accepted congratulations on his performance from an admiral in full dress uniform. Shuff registered a vague impression of the man's appearance. 'I love sailors!' he belched. Then his eyes focused on the admiral's ribbons. He peered woozily up at him and declared, 'My dear, you must have gone down on Nelson to cop that lot'.'

Comedian Billy Wells booked Rex for a summer season in 1964 at the Rainbow Room, Jersey, to co-star in *The Billy Wells Music Hall*. 'There was a stream not far from the stage door,' recalled Wells in 1979. 'Rex's digs were nearby and often after a show, and much the worse for wear, he would go home in costume. On several occasions he ended up in the stream in full drag, his wig askew and with bits of water weed dangling from his head. He looked like an elderly, drunken Ophelia.'

Magician John Wade, who was working in Jersey the same summer, remembered Wells' show: 'Rex started the season closing the bill, was swiftly moved to closing the second half and then to the opening but still managed to fall out of the circle bar and onto the stalls one night after he had done his opening spot. The duty free booze on the island was tempting for everyone.'

Producer Duggie Chapman recalled an ill-fated friendship between Rex and some Jersey fans. 'He became friendly with a husband and wife who had a house on the island and who were fans of his,' said Duggie. 'They had a daughter aged about twelve. One afternoon they suggested that Rex took the daughter down to the beach for a picnic. Rex took a bottle of Scotch with him — and the two of them drank it together. They had a whale of a time and got absolutely legless. I don't think, though, that he was ever asked round the house again.'

When I left the pub that night I'd got no money left and I had to walk home. It was about two and a half miles. And when I got to my turning I thought well, it's no good me charging in and having a scene with the old man because all he'll say is 'where have you been?', 'who have you been with?' and 'how much have you managed to spend?' So I thought what I'll do is to take all me clothes off downstairs and I'll sort of slide up and creep into the Chamber of Horrors and if he says anything I shall say 'I was watching the Epilogue and I nodded off'. So I got to my turning, I hadn't got a stitch on, and I was up the stairs and I got to the bit where it sort of turns round the bend at the top and I got the shock of my life. I was on top of a 29 bus! And all these people turned round, all sober. As if they had never seen a woman with no clothes on on top of a bus before. I just stood there. Well, I still had me earrings on. So it just goes to show what can happen after a half a glass of Christmas cake . . .

The Waterman's Arms

Music Hall had its roots in the smoky song and supper rooms that populated Britain in the 18th century. The rowdy audiences originally sat at tables and were encouraged to drink large amounts of alcohol while they watched

The Amazing Mrs Shufflewick

the star turns of the day perform. It was this Rabelaisian, bawdy atmosphere that the writer and TV interviewer Dan Farson tried to recreate when he opened the Waterman's Arms on the Isle of Dogs in 1962.

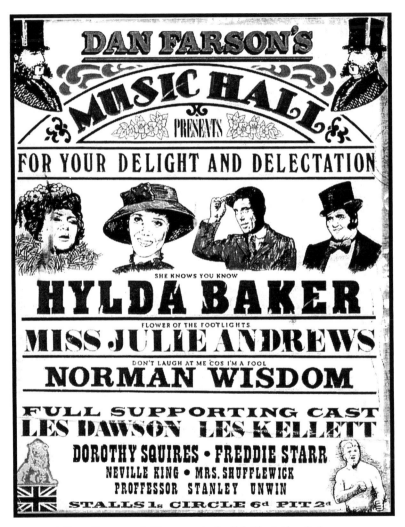

A Dan Farson sixties music hall bill at the Princes Theatre in London

Farson, gay and alcoholic, was a larger than life figure who was enormously popular on TV in the fifties and sixties. He was noted for investigating quirks, oddities and various forbidden facets of life (though not homosexuality) in programmes such as *Out of Step* and *Farson's Guide to the British*. He had arrived in London's East End in the late fifties, driven from his beloved Soho, by the impossibility of finding somewhere affordable to live, and to the East by the possibilities of finding a house by the river. He found a house by the Docklands area and discovered that not only was it Elizabethan but that it had once been a pub called the Waterman's Arms. It was a name that he was to co-opt for his business venture in 1962.

Part of Farson's grand plan for the Waterman's Arms (the former Newcastle Arms in Glengarnock Avenue) was to give a boost to the East End tradition of singing in pubs — the other was to revive the tradition of real music hall. When the Met in the Edgware Road was being demolished, he bought up the theatre's front box and two supporting caryatids which became part of the upstairs bar at the Watermans. He also bid at an auction at the old Collins Music Hall for a pastel of Harry Tate and a large portrait of Little Tich. The music hall impresario Don Ross provided a poster of Marie Lloyd on her final bill. All these artefacts were on display at the Waterman's, along with signed photographs of Trevor Howard, Adam Faith and Oliver Reed.

Thanks to Farson's journalistic skills the Waterman's opened in a blaze of publicity and, although the venture lasted only two rather shambolic years, the pub became world famous. The place was packed every night with celebrities — Lord Snowden, Kenneth Tynan, Clint Eastwood, Groucho Marx, Lady Diana Cooper, Judy Garland (who once got up and sang) and William Burroughs were just a few who were seen there.

Star performers at the pub were singers such as Ida Barr and Kim Cordell but it was Rex who appeared most frequently and drew the biggest crowds. For Mrs Shufflewick it was the ideal venue: a rowdy, boisterous, East End pub full of cockney characters. Mrs S could do no wrong. She was on home territory.

There were other acts who delighted the audiences — the man who sang *Mule Train* and banged his head with a tin tray, a docker who impersonated Frankenstein's monster, a taxi driver from the nearby Rising Sun pub who sang Al Jolson songs and a girl in spectacles, dressed with the severity of a city secretary, who was known as 'the white mouse' who sang so startlingly off-key that she was greeted with cheers whenever she appeared.

Rex recorded an album, *Look in at the Local* (1964), with Kim Cordell and Ida Barr, which was recorded live at the Watermans. Now a rarity, it is brilliant evocation of an extraordinary venue.

The same year Farson decided to present a similar type of entertainment on the West End stage. Together with then producer William Donaldson (later the author of the scurrilous *Henry Root Letters*) and the unlikely backing of maverick film director Michael Winner, he approached the impresario Bernard Delfont with the plan. Delfont controlled many West End theatres and Farson had his eye on the Comedy Theatre. Farson and Donaldson were seen by Delfont in his office.

'I explained my concept of a boisterous type of new music hall, rather than reconstruction with a chairman and hammer,' Farson recalled. 'I mentioned various artistes and Delfont stopped me sharply when I came to Mrs Shufflewick. 'No, he's wrong. He sends music hall up. Now the one artiste I was absolutely sure of was Mrs Shufflewick. 'I don't think that's fair,' I protested. 'Mrs Shufflewick is music hall.' Donaldson flinched, but Delfont pressed a switch on his intercom which connected him to his advisor Billy Marsh. 'What does the name Mrs Shufflewick mean to you?' he asked. 'If it's anything to do with music hall there is no one better, but . . .' 'Thanks,' said Delfont and turned to me. 'Alright then, go on'.

Nights at the Comedy starred Rex in second spot, the northern comic Jimmy James, Kim Cordell, a young Jimmy Tarbuck, and was compered by Manchester variety artiste Jacky Carlton. The show opened at the Comedy Theatre and was warmly received by the critics. Harold Hobson, then the doyenne of theatre critics, praised Mrs Shufflewick in *The Sunday Times* for timing her lines 'more skilfully than Mussolini did his trains,' adding that 'she is overwhelmingly and shatteringly funny. She manifests the heart-warming honest vulgarity we hear so much about. She is also very relevant to serious theatre.'

Unfortunately, the public stayed away in droves and the show closed in just three days. 'It folded because of lack of money,' said Rex. 'Dan was very happy-go-lucky, but not terribly good at business. He was a brilliant interviewer when he was on the top of his form. But then he used to get pissed every night and that was that.'

As both were heavy drinkers, Rex and Farson's friendship might be seen as a marriage made in heaven and although *Nights at the Comedy* had been a flop, Rex was undeterred and he and Farson often went out drinking in Soho, notably at the Colony Club.

The club, presided over by the harridan-like Nina Hammett and frequented by the likes of the artist, Francis Bacon, was once described by the art critic Richard Cork as 'a mixture of Soho bohemians, often with plummy people with broken noses, looking thuggish, but quite often gay.' The mixture fascinated Rex.

The Waterman's Arms closed with losses of £30,000 and, acting on impulse, Farson resigned his successful career on TV, abandoned his home on the river and retired to North Devon to write. He and Rex remained loyal friends for many years although in his later life Farson's alcoholism became so crippling that many were surprised that he survived to the age of 70. He knew he was dying of cancer in March 1997 when his compelling and self-deprecating autobiography, *Never a Normal Man*, was published. Held in much affection by his friends, only Rex remained unsurprised by his often erratic behaviour.

Rex starred in another West End music hall venture, a one-off at the Princes Theatre in 1965, which boasted a top cast including Julie Andrews, Norman Wisdom, Hylda Baker, Stanley Unwin and Dorothy Squires. The same year he was back on television in *Let's Laugh*, a BBC series which highlighted three different club acts each week. He appeared in one episode with the comedians Hope and Keen and the impressionist Mike Yarwood.

He decided to drop Joe Collins as his agent and for a period in the sixties was managed by the Riscoe agency. 'When Joe Collins signed me up for £40 a week in variety

I thought I was doing well,' said Rex. 'I didn't think about all the travel expenses and all that. I just had stars in my eyes — until I discovered that he was getting £150 a week for me. I couldn't believe it.'

The Riscoe agency booked him regularly on the Butlin's holiday camp circuit where he topped the bills on Sunday night concerts. The family audiences were appreciative, many of them recognising Mrs S from radio and television, but his repertoire was constrained. In every Butlin's dressing room there was an imposing sign: 'May we remind artistes that Butlin's cater for family audiences – and despite the permissive world outside we intent to maintain our standards. Blue material is unacceptable at Butlin's'.

He also appeared in the occasional pantomime, always as the Dame, and always billed as Mrs Shufflewick. There was no mention in the programmes of Rex Jameson. The Riscoe agency had also changed his billing matter — Mrs S was no longer 'TV and Radio's Greatest Laugh', she was now 'Radio and TV's most curious character'.

This is a letter I've had from my youngest boy, my Ernie. I wish you could see my other boy, young Nigel. He's the one with the brains; he takes after me you see. He's only 19 and as young as that boy is he is now being detained to give Her Majesty pleasure. So she must think something of him. Anyway, this is from my Ernie. He says, 'Dear Sir or Madam, I am writing this very slow because I know you cannot read very quick. I have got so many different holes in my socks I can put them on fourteen different ways. Out here life is one long round of picnics, parties and balls. The week

*before last it was all picnics, last week it was all
parties, and this week it has all been cancelled.'
I can't follow the next bit. He says 'I would have
put two pounds in for you but I have stuck the
envelope down.' Takes after his father in that
bit. Whoever he was. Never even took his cap off.
And I was eating chips at the time. And then he
finishes up 'May gawd keep you from your loving
son, Ernie'. I think it's Ernie. Or Elsie.*

*I'm glad I've only got my two boys to worry
about. I mean you can't be too sure these days,
can you? All these sexual changes going on. You
send your kids abroad, Switzerland, there's a
start. Two pills and a nick with a fish knife and
you never know what's coming home . . .*

On the Move

Rex had always endured the camaraderie of variety, backstage banter and travelling on trains with fellow artistes.
Roy Hudd recalled working with him in the sixties: 'I did
variety with him and remember him going into a pub full of
dour, hard-drinking Carlisle blokes and shouting, 'Finish
your drinks, we're going to have an orgy!' One of the short-
est train journeys I've ever had was from Penzance (we'd
been doing a *Workers' Playtime*) to London, overnight.
Rex got the booze out and myself, Rex and Anita Harris
didn't stop laughing till the train pulled into London.'

Comedian Johnny Dallas was on a variety bill with Rex
at the Theatre Royal Hanley. 'We both finished early and
caught the same train back to London on the Saturday
night,' he said. 'The journey started well with long dis-
cussions about pros and the business but as the journey

progressed so did Rex's drinking. By the time we arrived in London he could hardly stand. I helped him to a taxi but the cabbie didn't want to take him. Then Rex pulled himself up and grandly announced, 'Tis I, your mother — take me home!' and the cabbie, recognising him, said, 'Bloody hell, it's Mrs Shufflewick, pour him in!' and off they went.'

Clubs

The mid-sixties saw the rise of clubland in Britain and working men's clubs sprung up all around the country. The north dominated the circuit with giant clubs in Yorkshire and Lancashire, many of them owning their own breweries and casinos. As variety theatres closed many entertainers were forced to work in clubland, some successfully, others much less so. 'They were, in a sense, the halls all over again in the setting of the nightclubs of the north,' observed comedian Max Wall who became one of clubland's top attractions.

Comedian Max Wall, friend and drinking partner of Rex

Rex was reluctant to take Mrs S out into the northern clubs — he had never liked playing northern variety but financially he had no choice. Nevertheless, Mrs S, now considerably more rude and light years away from her scatterbrained radio original, proved popular with the punters. Like the Waterman's Arms, the raucous, boozy atmosphere seemed a natural setting for a Mrs S monologue.

But even in clubland eyebrows were sometimes raised: 'I've had one or two concert secretaries who thought the act was near the knuckle but I don't think I've ever had any complaints from the audience,' said Rex. 'Only once or twice in Wales where you get a lot of those chapel people. Women respond even more than men. They laugh louder and applaud longer. I never look a clubland audience in the face. I always look above their heads into space. I think if you were looking at their faces and they were a bit glum, it would put you off.'

Working the clubs, like variety, meant that for long periods Rex was rootless. He had no permanent base in London and lived for most of the time in a succession of digs or cheap rented flats. 1967 found him based in Nottingham where he struck up another unlikely friendship, this time with the Hollywood screen actor Robert Ryan who was appearing in a season at the Nottingham Playhouse as James Tyrone in *Long Day's Journey into Night* and *Othello*. Best known in films for playing rugged western types and war heroes, Ryan was also an acclaimed stage actor with a deep love of theatre. He and Rex would sometimes meet in the Playhouse bar at lunchtimes. 'He talked a lot about Broadway and vaudeville,' said Rex, 'and I talked to him about films and music hall. He was a very intelligent man.'

I've often thought of Rex and Robert Ryan boozing together during those lunchtimes and wondered what Ryan's evening performances of *Long Day's Journey* or *Othello* were really like.

Without doubt Rex's nomadic existence contributed to his alcoholism. When the boozing had finished in his dressing room, it continued in the nearest bar. And when the bar closed he usually went back to his digs alone. Sometimes there were casual pickups, rough trade or one night stands. Rex thought they would lead to something else, a permanent relationship perhaps.

Drink and gambling took their toll financially as well as affecting his working reputation. Managements in regional theatres and clubs began to be wary of booking Mrs S and by the end of the sixties he had been quietly dropped by the Riscoe agency. William Owen remembers seeing Rex perform at the Civic Theatre, Barnsley: 'He was top of the bill and was required to do two spots in each half. His first spot went well but during the interval he had obviously had a few. The stage manager managed to steer him to the centre behind the tabs. The curtains opened and Rex proceeded to entertain the audience. Unfortunately, it was the same spot as he had just done in the first half.'

Although he was a boozer there was never any doubt about Rex's comic talent and, like other great variety performers such as Frankie Howerd and Max Wall, he appealed to intellectuals as well as variety and club audiences. In 1969 he did a two week season at the Royal Court Theatre in London. 'They were a good audience at the Royal Court,' he reflected. 'A little higher class than the usual club audiences, but better if anything. They laughed just as much at the blue bits.'

In 1968 Roger Baker published his seminal book on female impersonation, *Drag*, in which he compared Rex to Dan Leno and Old Mother Riley (Arthur Lucan). Rex attended the book launch at the Horseshoe Hotel in London along with many other drag artistes. Variety artiste Bernard Maeder recalled the occasion: 'My partner Andy and I were there along with Roy Alvis and Danny O'Dell, Barri Chatt and Terry Gardener. Billy Wells was there and so was Lee Sutton. Lee had been on television a few days before, stating that because he did drag, it did not mean he was gay and he was, in fact, a very virile heterosexual. Lee asked Billy is he could use one of his numbers. Billy replied it wouldn't be any good for him, as to do the piece properly he would need feathers up his arse. Lee said, 'Well, I've had everything else up there so a few feathers won't hurt!'

Meeting Mrs Shufflewick

I was just 15 in 1969 when I first saw Mrs Shufflewick. I was working part-time in the Unicorn Bookshop in Brighton, famed in the sixties as one of Britain's first 'alternative', or rather 'underground', bookshops. It was run by the American poet Bill Butler and his partner, Michael Hughes, a former theatre director.

One day shortly before Christmas, Michael said to me, 'Ring up the Co-operative Hall. There's an adult panto-mime on there called *Sinderella* starring Mrs Shufflewick. Check and see if she's on tonight and Bill and I will take you to see the show.'

I laughed out loud. Mrs Shufflewick? I'd never heard of her. What a daft name. I thought Michael was pulling my leg.

'Don't be silly,' I said. 'There's no such person.'

He smiled. 'Mrs Shufflewick is Rex Jameson. He's a very funny comic. You'll love him. The only thing is, he's often pissed. That's why I want to know if he's on tonight.'

I rang the Co-op Hall and a lady assured me that Mrs S would definitely be performing. I booked three seats but was still convinced I was being set up. Someone was playing a joke on me.

Sinderella was the most outrageous and filthy pantomime I had ever seen in my life. I had seen several pantomimes as a child, including two starring the great Irish comedian Jimmy O'Dea, but nothing had prepared me for the sight of Mrs Shufflewick. Red nosed, tipsy, unbelievably bawdy, yet somehow genteel and refined, she was a law unto herself. Whenever she came on stage all eyes were upon her. Mrs S, as Cinderella with an S, gin soaked and past her prime, could do no wrong with the audience that night. She hoicked up her skirts, swore and ad-libbed. The audience adored her. They wolf-whistled, clapped and cheered.

By the interval she was sozzled and by the second half legless. When the rest of the cast came on for the finale she was nowhere to be seen. 'We want Shuff!' the audience chanted — but to no avail. Mrs S had passed out in the dressing room cold.

Bill, Michael and I left the theatre, laughing, joking and recounting every one of Mr's S's gags all the way home. 'I told you that you would love Mrs Shufflewick,' said Michael. Love her? I was hooked.

Postscript: There were so many complaints about the blue material used during the show that the police banned the panto and it closed after two nights.

Rex, backstage in the 1960s with variety star Ethel Revnell of the comedy duo Revnell and West, 'The Cockney Kids'.

PART TWO

Getting to Know Rex

The upstairs bar of the Horseshoe Hotel in London's Tottenham Court Road was faded and shabby. Worn carpets, red flock wallpaper. Cigarette ash covered the floor. The tables were adorned with cheap glass ashtrays filled with salty peanuts.

On a Tuesday evening in the early seventies, The British Music Hall Society held their monthly meetings and cabaret shows here, presided over by impresario Don Ross, once married to 'Nellie Dean' star Gertie Gitana. Mrs Shufflewick was a regular turn at the BMHS shows and one night in 1972 I went along to catch the act.

This sailor came up to me and he said 'Excuse me, I know you won't mind me saying this, but you do remind me of Elizabeth Taylor.' I thought, hello, me luck's changed here. I said 'Well, that's very kind of you, is it my figure ?' He said 'Yes, it's gone for a Burton.'

'So what's Mrs Shufflewick like in real life?' I asked Don Ross, who sat opposite me in an immaculate black suit. No creases. 'Why don't you go and ask himself yourself?' said Don briskly. 'He's over there standing at the bar. But he'll cost you. He drinks like a fish.'

There at the bar was a tiny figure just over four foot tall, dressed in a shabby mac, a pair of baggy trousers that looked as if they were held up by string, a Chairman Mao hat perched on his head and an ill-fitting toupee underneath that was slipping. I looked closer and saw a red wizened face with traces of greasepaint at the edges, enormous large blue round eyes like pools, a cigarette dangled from his lips. He looked like a pixie who had fallen on hard times.

I gingerly approached him. 'Excuse me, are you Mrs Shufflewick?'

The figure turned round sharply, surprised and amused at the interruption. At six foot I towered over him.

'Yes,' he slurred slightly.

'Can I buy you a drink? I'm a great admirer of your act.'

'My dear,' he said, suddenly arching himself up elegantly. 'That's a splendid idea. Make it a large Scotch.'

That was my first meeting with Rex. I had seen him perform in theatres and gay bars and I had heard some of his recordings. I was hooked on him but had never approached him at any stage door. We talked briefly about his career and I told him a bit about myself. At the time I was an actor and was just in the process of starting up a comedy double act with another actor, Richard Ruck. I bought Rex more drinks. He asked for my telephone number. I

Richard Ruck (left) and the author as 70s double act, Ruck and Newley. Rex used to write gags for us.

thought for a moment he wanted to pick me up. Alarmed as I was by the idea of being seduced by an alcoholic pixie, I obliged. He smiled, said nothing more and left.

At seven o'clock the next morning my telephone rang. 'It's Rex here. Shuff. Do you want to go for a drink? We'll meet at the Fitzroy, off Tottenham Court Road, at eleven. There's no point in hanging around is there?'

Eleven o'clock and Rex was already outside the pub waiting for the doors to open. He was still standing in the same baggy suit, the Mao cap with the toupee askew, and the eternal Woodbine dangling from his mouth. This was the start of a routine that was to become familiar to me over the years. The early morning call, the first joke of the day (always a new one), the meeting in a pub. The locations changed according to his mood. If relatively sober, he'd want to meet up somewhere smart and central — The Captain's Cabin off the Haymarket or Harry's Bar at the Regent Palace Hotel ('My dear, you get free olives there and a paper tissue as a drinks mat') and, if drunk, somewhere grotty, a dingy dive, usually Irish and often in Kentish Town. Drinking with Rex was like playing alcoholic musical chairs.

Conversations would begin with a betting prediction, then maybe a gag inspired by one of the newspapers he had picked up along the way from the pavement or a dustbin and then stories about his career. His comments on fellow artistes were varied. He loved all the people who were known as awkward or difficult. The more tempestuous they were the more he spoke of them with affection. Dorothy Squires, Charles Hawtrey, Hylda Baker, Joan Turner — none of them could do any wrong. Others did not fare as well. Jack Douglas — 'as funny as a burning orphanage' and various BBC producers — 'bastards, some of them.'

The morning sessions sometimes progressed into the afternoon, by which time Rex was so drunk I had to take him back to his flat in Kentish Town by taxi. Most people would have been deeply shocked by his living conditions. Situated on the first floor of 25 Falkland Road, the flat consisted of just two damp rooms and a kitchen. He was virtually a squatter and hadn't paid the rent for years. The wallpaper was peeling and the furniture was falling to pieces.

The carpets were moulding and above all there was a terrible stench of urine, stale cigarettes and drink permeating every part of the flat. On my first visit, my immediate reaction was to vomit. There were battered suitcases containing Mrs S's costumes and old BBC Radio scripts. The kitchen was piled high with washing up and rotting food. The bath was stacked with old bits of iron and a bucket. It hadn't been used for years and one day Rex said to me, in all honesty: 'It is my proud boast that I have never taken a bath in 23 years, and I don't intend to start now. Perish the thought.' This was Rex's home, his private world and one that very few people ever saw.

One day, in a call from a public phone box, Rex said to me: 'You know you ought to be my manager. You know things about me. Besides, you've got a telephone. I haven't. You can start now.' As the pips ran out I became Mrs Shufflewick's personal manager.

Getting 'down and dirty'

This sailor did something I have never seen anyone do in a public house before and I hope I never shall again if I live to be thirty-two. He suddenly, without a word of warning, whipped out this packet of picture postcards wot he'd brought back from the Middle East and, quite honestly, I have never seen anything so disgusting — have you seen them? My gawd, they make your toes curl. Fifty-eight different ways to shake hands. And they're all in Agfa-Colour. How those people get themselves into those positions. Well, I couldn't. I've never been asked. No, but honestly, they are going a bit far. There's all these women with no clothes on, it's disgusting, and there's all these fellas with even less. Bless 'em. And they've got themselves in this attitude, with one leg on the mantlepiece and the other

in the coal bucket. And they don't seem to talk
at all. Well, I know it's rude to speak with your
mouth full . . . no, I mean you'd think they'd say
something. I gave them back to him after three
quarters of an hour. I put my magnifying glass
back in my handbag and I said 'I have no wish
to look at this type of literature, thank you very
much, as far as I'm concerned you can get behind
me Satan.' And do you know those were the worst
few words . . .

By the time I had met Rex in 1972 Mrs S was pickled, sour and almost dangerous. Freed from the restraints of broadcasting and family entertainment, she was able to be as down and dirty as she pleased. Gone was *Variety Bandbox*'s innocent cockney chatterbox. Mrs S now resembled Hogarth's drink-sodden mother abandoning her baby in the famous cartoon *Gin Lane*.

Furthermore, she and Rex began to merge into one. Rex talked and drank like Mrs S. Mrs S talked and drank like Rex. And few people called Rex by his christian name anymore; he was simply known as Shuff.

In the early seventies he was openly gay for the first time in his life and much of his work was in the many gay bars and clubs that had sprung up in London which presented drag shows every night. Pubs like the Black Cap in Camden Town (a sign above the door read 'The Palladium of Drag'), The Vauxhall Tavern (where Paul O'Grady's viperous Lily Savage was born), The Union Tavern and The Skinner's Arms in Camberwell, were all heaving with crowds eager to see the likes of Marc Fleming, an acid tongued and barbed drag performer with brilliant humour, Lee Sutton who reigned supreme at the Union Tavern where he recorded an LP, *Drag for Camp Followers*, and the huge, grossly overweight Canadian, Jean Fredericks, who blew a trombone and gave 'recitals' in a sequined dress.

There was also a multitude of crass mime acts in drag pretending to be Dorothy Squires, Shirley Bassey or Alma Cogan, wildly flaying their arms and mouthing the words to heartbreak torch songs and leaving the stage to the sound of their own footsteps, the only thing that was real in what was a strange, surreal world.

In the middle of all this, Mrs S stood out like a 200 carat diamond, a real variety performer, whose professional approach was almost out of place in such surroundings. Yet gay audiences were hugely loyal towards Rex and were often some of the best he had ever played to, despite the fact that many were too young to have known of his variety career. 'The music hall started in pubs and that's where it's finished up now,' he said. 'I get my best audiences in pubs. I do twenty minutes, you get a great audience, and it's marvellous.' He was not happy, however, with many of the supporting acts: 'I like the drag pubs, but not the mime acts,' he said. 'They put on a record and a frock and they think this is an act. I've always tried to be a comedian, make them laugh.'

The Comeback

Being Rex's manager was no easy task. In the gay pubs he had an enormous following but unfortunately the generosity of some of his fans in sending round bottles of Guinness, often cruelly laced with vodka, gin or whiskey, had disastrous effects and he would sometimes forget a whole routine. Audiences took their chances with him. When he was on top form there were few comics to equal his timing or sense of the absurd. When he was drunk he was awful. But you couldn't hide drink from him. He was an alcoholic divining rod. He knew exactly where to find booze.

What shocked me most when I first began to manage him was just how little he was earning. Gone were the days when he was earning three or four figures a week, he was now being paid as little as ten pounds per date in the gay clubs. A bottle of whiskey was sometimes thrown in. Sometimes he would perform just for the whiskey. It occurred to me that the only way to up the wages was to put him somewhere at the top of the showbusiness ladder in one fell swoop. Remembering his affection for the singer Dorothy Squires, and also her penchant for hiring the London Palladium to suit herself and her campy fans, I dropped her a letter at her home in Bray. Would she take a chance on Rex in a Palladium show? I wondered.

The answer came quickly in a loud and raucous phone call from the lady herself. 'Ill tell you what I'll fucking do,' she rasped in rapid Welsh tones, "I'm doing the fucking Lewisham Odeon next month. If Rex behaves himself on stage, and I mean fucking behaves, then I will give him a chance at the Palladium.' She slammed down the phone. She was obviously pissed.

Lewisham Odeon on a Sunday night passed without a hitch. Comedian Roy Walker opened the bill and was followed by Rex. Squires occupied the second half. Afterwards an American fan knocked on Rex's door and said: 'Gee, I must meet that fine, fine lady. She is such a gas.' It was the singer Johnny Ray, convinced that Rex was some

The volatile performer Dorothy Squires who booked Rex on several occasions to appear with her at the London Palladium

eccentric old lady. Rex didn't break the spell and gave a small curtsey, blushed, and then offered his cheek for a kiss. He got it.

The first London Palladium show followed shortly after and I fed various newspapers the news that Rex was on the bill. The show was a sell-out and there were as many people there to see Rex as there were fans of Dot, most of whom were in feathers and sequins and looked exactly like the lady herself. Barbara Cartland sat in the Royal Box with Danny La Rue, prompting one old queen in the stalls to ask, 'Which one's which?' Rex opened the show and did forty minutes. At the end he got a standing ovation. He was on stage where he belonged.

From that one Palladium date I was able to up his fees immediately and within a month he was the highest paid performer on the gay pub circuit. The odd variety bookings started to come in and he appeared in smart clubs such as the Country Cousins in the Kings Road alongside acts such as Bertice Reading and Hinge and Bracket. The Young Vic Theatre even rang up one day and suggested he do monologues by Samuel Beckett. 'No,' said Rex. 'I couldn't remember the words. I'd look like an old fool.' A pity. Beckett would have loved him.

Not everyone knew who Mrs Shufflewick was. I once rang the James Russell Agency who specialised in floor shows and adult entertainment in the hope that there might be the odd date for Rex. The agency was run by a loud speaking black man. After I had given a long list of Mrs Shufflewick's variety and club credits there was a pause. 'Dat's OK man,' said the voice, 'but does she do de strip?'

I went to see my doctor the other night. Dr McKankie. He was sitting there at his desk with his horn rimmed glasses on and his ball point in his hand and he said, 'Come in, dear.' He treats me just as if I'm human. He said, 'Have you had a check-up lately?' I said, 'No, a couple of Hungarians.' I knew I shouldn't have said it. Still, the devil was in me that night. Or someone with a red hat on. He said, 'Well, take off all your clothes and I'll examine your ears.' You feel such a fool stuck there with nothing on. You don't know where to put your hands for the best. If you cover the swings, you lose on the roundabouts. I put mine behind me head. Then he said, 'I want you to do something for me if you will.' And I said, 'Yes, by all means,' and he went over and pulled the blinds down. I thought, hello, this is where you get struck off. And he came back with this sort of torch thing and he said, 'I want you to cross your legs as a precaution.' Do you know he gave me such as bash with this blessed rubber hammer and you know your leg is supposed to jump up – well, mine fell off. He said, 'Well, get your clothes on then, I can't find out what's wrong with you. I think it must be the drink.' So I said, 'Well, I'm not bothered Doctor, I can come back when you're sober.'

Dot Squires booked the Palladium again in 1976 and asked Rex to share the bill. He was almost blasé about the prospect and pretended it was 'just another date.' Come the day the show was sold out again and there were a lot of old queens outside the box office shouting at each other. There was a rehearsal going on inside and people shouting there too. Rex hadn't turned up. When he did arrive in the dressing room, not long before curtain up, he had two carrier bags. One had the costume and the bigger one was stacked with booze. He sat down at the dressing table, lit a fag and started making-up.

'Why all the fuss?' he said, turning to me. 'I've been doing this act for thirty years. Nobody ever rehearsed in variety anyway.' He peered into a carrier bag and brought out a bottle of Scotch.

'Don't worry,' he said smugly, 'I'm only having the one.' My face broke into a nervous smile.

'Five minutes please, Mr Jameson, five minutes.' That was the tannoy. We went up the stairs and into the wings. Rex seemed nervous. There were over 2,000 people out there.

He looked at me and there were drops of sweat dribbling down his make-up. Then a voice announced, 'Ladies and Gentlemen, Mrs Shufflewick!' and there was a roar from the audience. He was on.

His ten minute spot ran to eighteen and the audience loved it, especially when he looked up at the ornate theatre ceiling and said, 'Look at the fucking dust up there.'

Unfortunately Dot had been standing in the wings and overheard the remark. As Rex came off to loud applause, battling Dot ran towards me and grabbed me by the arm.

'Mr Newley!' she screamed, 'Let me tell you this, nobody, but nobody, swears on my fucking stage!' and as she pushed me, I nearly fell down the stairs. In the dressing room Rex said he wasn't going to bother to come on at the finale. 'There's no point,' he said. 'I'll go round the front and watch Dot's act.' In which case, I told him, I would go home, and we arranged to meet at the Black Cap the next day.

At 11.00am Rex was sitting in the bar reading *The Sporting Life* and drinking a barley wine mixed with Guinness.

'So how did it all finish up?' I asked brightly.

'It didn't,' said Rex slowly.

'Oh no, tell me what happened,' I said.

'Well, it's like this. I drank the rest of the whiskey and got changed into me normal clothes and staggered around to the front of the theatre. I told the doorman I was Mrs Shufflewick and that I'd just got a standing ovation and I wanted to see the rest of the show.'

'And what did he say?' I asked.

'He told me to fuck off and threw me down the steps.' He burped loudly. 'You know I bet that's never happened to anyone who's just played the London Palladium, has it?' he asked.

'No, Rex,' I said. 'I don't suppose it has.'

I felt shocking when we came out of that pub. Well, I say came out — we were asked to leave. It was him messin' about. He's had a couple of these pills, I think he said they were 'coming on' pills. And he's had these two and he was rampant. He was jigging up and down and twanging my knicker elastic and throwing his pension book in the air as if there was no tomorrow. I don't remember leaving the pub. I know I had my head on his shoulder. I forget who was holding me feet.

Mates and Models

Rex's own taste in comedy was simple. Throughout the seventies he continued to visit the cinema, often in the West End where cinema managers — some of them Black Cap regulars — knew him and would give him a free ticket. He loved his 'Carry On' films but bemoaned the passing of vintage Hollywood comedies. 'I'm sorry to sound like Mary Whitehouse,' he said, 'but you don't get great comedies these days. I like to go and see a film and have a damn good laugh.'

He admired various comedians such as Les Dawson but his favourite remained Frankie Howerd. 'Frankie makes me laugh,' he said. 'Now there's a man I could sit and scream at with laughter all night. Frankie's stuff is all down to earth — it's situation comedy.'

Frankie and he were friends, as was Max Wall who he occasionally met up with for a mutual Guinness. Other favourite comics he had known included the famous drag duos Ford and Sheen and Bartlett and Ross, both of whom he talked about when I got him an appearance on *Looks Familiar*, Dennis Norden's popular TV nostalgia show.

One performer whom he admired, but had not previously met, was Douglas Byng, whom he had first seen in the theatre in the musical *The Bird Seller* at the Palace Theatre in 1947. One of the 20th century's most redoubtable entertainers, Byng's long career had spanned musical comedy, revue, pantomime, cabaret and television. Billed as 'Bawdy But British', he was a prolific songwriter and a master of the double entendre, often appearing in female guise as either a noted pantomime Dame or as a cabaret star in London's glittering nightclubs during the 1930s. Noel Coward once described his act as 'the most refined vulgarity in London'. Dougie lived and worked to the remarkable age of 94, his last appearance being his one man show which I directed at the National Theatre in 1987

I managed Dougie, as he was fondly known, for the last fifteen years of his life, when he was much in demand as a raconteur on television. Although he and Rex could not have been more different in personality or appearance – Dougie was highly sophisticated and immaculately dressed at all times, Rex was more down to earth and usually dressed like a tramp — they got on well when I introduced them to each other.

They first met at a charity function at a London hotel. Dougie, who looked rather like George Burns with a monocle, wore a green velvet suit and sipped dry sherry. Rex, for once sporting a tie with his baggy jacket and trousers, gulped neat Scotch. Both seemed apprehensive. I broke the ice and mentioned panto dames. Dougie admired George Lacey and Danny La Rue. Rex liked Norman Evans. They both smiled.

Dougie lived in an elegant Regency flat on Brighton's seafront and sometimes when Rex was playing a Brighton club I would take him along to see Dougie. As time went on they got to know each other and the friendship warmed. Rex was more relaxed and even took to visiting Dougie on his own. In the comfort of his flat Dougie drank pink champagne. But he always kept a bottle of Guinness in a cupboard especially for Rex.

Rex . . . the cook

When Rex was sober he liked cooking and eating. He had very traditional tastes and at his dilapidated flat in Kentish Town he used to make meat stews or pies. He prided himself on making home made dumplings and scotch eggs.

When he was out on his daily travels around Kentish and Camden Town or the West End he would often drop into a greasy spoon. Spaghetti bolognaise was his favourite. He always had a sweet tooth and if he was passing a bakery would buy a donut or a couple of gingerbread men.

When he came round to my house he used to ask for cheese on toast or 'Welsh rabbit' as he called it. He always carried a quarter bottle of Scotch in his pocket and when I made him a coffee he would pour a drop into his cup.

Billy Wells once told me that he invited Rex round for a day at his house in Fulham and that Rex had insisted on cooking lunch. Billy had to go out shopping for an hour or two and left him in the kitchen. Far from sober and swigging Guinness, Rex managed to cobble something together on the stove but then passed out cold in the living room.

'When I got back the kitchen was in flames,' said Billy. 'That's the sort of thing that happened if you asked 'Madam' around.'

Pure Corn

The cockney comedian Chubby Oates was one of Rex's closest friends. An ebullient clubland performer and a panto dame who boasted a 54" bosom, he was for many years a stalwart of the *Paul Raymond Revues*. He recalled that at the start of his career, when working as a junior reporter on a local newspaper, he had been sent to interview Rex at a provincial theatre:

'Far from being the imposing figure I expected, he was charming — but instead of an interview he sent me down to the local butchers to get a pound of lard as he had nothing to remove his make-up with.'

Chubby and Rex had worked together on many variety bills and clubs during the sixties but were memorably teamed together when they became an integral part of the infamous *Pure Corn* shows that were something of a fixture at the Theatre Royal, Stratford East in the late seventies.

The shows were originally the idea of the comedian Lee Tracey, and were envisaged as a kind of anarchic, rumbus-

THEATRE ROYAL, STRATFORD, E.15
01-534 0310

★ **VARIETY** ★

Thurs   March 21 st   8 pm

MAX WALL v MRS. SHUFFLEWICK

Fri March 22nd   8 pm

HINGE & BRACKET v RITA WEBB

Sat   March 23rd 8 pm

ROGERS & STARR

Sun. March 24th at 7.30 pm

BARBARA WINDSOR plus
'Arnold Capper' JOHN HALSTEAD

each night a supporting team from   Larry Barnes (Escapologist)   Karl Dallas
the lovely Diane Langton   Kent Baker & Tony Locantro in the bar
Ken Hill   Sue Potter   Ron Hackett   Gaye Brown   Sandra Caron
Ian Armit's Music   Book Now If You Want a Seat

tious music hall, drag and stag show rolled into one. The scripts were corny, often blue and very topical, and were usually written by both Chubby and Rex. The stock company included Lee Tracey, Chubby, Rex, Tommy Osborne and sex-change Jennifer Scott and there were also appearances from then up and coming performers such as Bobby Davro and Michael Barrymore.

Bobby Davro, one of the up and coming stars of the ribald *Pure Corn* shows at the Theatre Royal Stratford East in the 1970s

'We did the shows on a shoestring,' said Chubby. 'They were always sold out well in advance and Rex was always the big draw. We always had to find new sketches for him; the audiences expected it. On one show he came on as a nun, another as a sally army majorette. He also came on as a ballerina and did the balloon dance with Lee. We used to do a lot of take-offs of TV shows like *What's My Line*. I remember him guessing the object in that. 'Is it a rosy, pink nipple?' he said loudly.

'He was usually pissed by the second half on most shows but that just added to the whole mayhem of the thing. He got bigger laughs than anyone else and it was difficult to follow him.'

Pure Corn shows were rehearsed a month in advance and played for just the one night at Stratford. On the day of the show itself I virtually had to keep Rex on a leash. He had so much new material to remember that it would have been fatal to have let him out of my sight. He used to spend the day at my house in South London and we would watch films while he had just a few bottles of Guinness. Every few hours Lee Tracey would ring me and gingerly ask, 'Is Madam sober?' 'Just about,' I'd reply.

Late afternoon we would take a taxi to Stratford East and when I had finally got Rex into his dressing room Lee would sigh with relief. I had delivered the goods.

I was reading one of these women's magazines last week and there was a whole page devoted to the stars and the occult. It's written by a gypsy fella. He lives in a field with a horse. It's a mare, so he knows what he's doing. He's got a glass eye and a crystal ball what he looks into. And he can tell you what you're going to do before you've done it. And then you write to him and he gets you out of it. There's one woman who wrote this letter. She said 'Dear Gypsy Pea, my husband has recently retired at the age of sixty-two and he is pottering about the house all day and all he can think of is — you know. I cannot bend down to plug in my Hoover or do any low dusting

but what he takes advantage. The house is in a
shocking state and my nerves are shot to pieces.'
And she'd signed herself 'Worried'. And then she
put 'PS, Please excuse the jerky handwriting.'

Sunday Lunch at The Black Cap

By far the most popular venue that Rex played was The Black Cap in Camden Town. Although it was then, and still is, one of London's most famous gay bars it attracted a large number of foreign tourists many of whom came to see its famous drag shows.

The Cap, as it is known, was then a typical seventies London gay entertainment pub. A Hammond organ and drums took pride of place on a tiny stage and a glitter ball twirled around to the sounds of Gloria Gaynor and Donna Summer while burly, moustachioed men in check shirts eyed each other up. The beer was extortionately priced — and lousy with it. You took your pick, a warm pint of Red Barrel or a flat Harp lager.

The interior walls were adorned with prints of famous panto Dames such as Clarkson Rose and Arthur Askey (both of whom would probably have died of shock if they'd ever walked into the place) but the biggest photograph was one of Mrs S that towered over the bar.

Rex always appeared on Sunday lunchtimes and attracted the biggest crowds, many of whom were pros, like Barry Cryer, Charles Hawtrey or Barry Humphries, who had come to catch his act. Rex had a love/hate relationship with the pub. The money was terrible — £15 a session and the then landlord refused to put the fee up — but the audiences were marvellous.

Rex held most drag pub landlords in contempt. 'They're doing it for the money,' he said. 'If they didn't make money and get the houses then they'd throw the whole drag thing out tomorrow night. They'd stick a disco on instead.'

He did two spots on Sunday lunchtimes, one solo and the other an impromptu double with Marc Fleming. Neither of them had any idea

Fellow drag performer, Barry Humphries, often came to see Rex's act at the Black Cap in Camden Town

what they would do or say in advance but both would arrive in the dressing room before the show with a newspaper in hand. Together they would glance at the stories and pick on a theme for the spot. Marc was an aggressive, quick witted comic, Rex, a lighter, more throwaway performer. They worked well together on stage but rarely socialised off. 'I like working with Marc,' said Rex. 'There's not many people I could work with, I must say that. Not because I didn't like them, because you've got to have the same sort of mental thing. You see, I can get up with Marc, and without any rehearsal we can do a quarter of an hour of comedy, just playing off the cuff, backwards and forwards to each other. Like someone playing tennis — I couldn't do that with everybody.'

For many punters Mrs S's Sunday shows were a regular date. 'It rather frightens me when you see the same people every time you're on,' said Rex. 'I think they must know what I'm going to say. I've got about five acts I do. I know these people who come in every week; they know the gags backwards — they still laugh, but I'd rather have people that haven't seen me before.'

I always thought the regulars were great. If Rex was drunk, they would chant the gags along with him.

Things have got so bad lately I'thought I'd have to go out to work. I went down to the labour exchange last week and there's this old cow behind the counter. She said 'Shufflewick, have you got your cards?' So I said, 'As a matter of fact I have,' so we had a quick game of pontoon and I lost. She said 'What's your profession?' I said, 'I'm a Coronation programme seller.' So she said 'Well, can you do anything else?' I said 'I'm very good at milking yaks.' She said 'I think we're going to have a problem with you.' So I sat down and this other woman came in through the door, dressed in a two piece and the brogues and a deerstalker hat and a pipe and she said, 'Ah, my good woman, are you looking for work?' I said, 'Well, as a matter of fact I am.' She said, '

I'm from the women's lib. If they find you a job we fight the case.'

Shortly before I first met him, Rex had made an LP which was recorded live at the Cap. The album, *A Drop of the Hard Shuff*, contained many of his key routines and shows him at his very best. But the album's popularity was, bizarrely, to prove detrimental to him. It became a favourite with comedians and drag acts throughout the country and within months of its release there were several performers — including one or two names — who were doing Rex's full act in clubs and theatres. There was little he could do. Jokes are not copyright but it seemed a cruel irony that many of the performers who had literally stolen Rex's act — an act that had been honed in variety for over three decades — should often go on to earn more than he did. Plagiarism is a game that any number can play.

This fella and me, we were just standing on the pavement outside the pub, just talking about this and that. I don't know what I said to upset him — I know I mentioned the price of plums — but he suddenly went berserk and made a lunge at me. Well, I don't know if you've ever been lunged at outside a pub at eleven o'clock in the evening but it's a shocking feeling. I did the first thing that came into me head. I shot down this side turning which I thought was an escape route and it turned out to be a cul-de-sac. And I'm stood there with me back to the brick wall and me legs in two dustbins with a John West salmon tin where it mattered most — with the lid up. And there's him with his good conduct medals clanking away and

*his string vest at half mast, I thought, this is it
tonight Gladys, Death or Dishonour. And then I
thought, well, I'm not bleedin' dying yet.*

The dressing room at the Cap was a tip. Stuck out behind
the back of the pub near the gents toilets and dustbins
the place stank. Inside there was a stone floor which was
freezing in winter. A cracked mirror hung precariously
above a makeshift dressing table. A couple of grotty stools
were thrown in for good measure. 'And they call this the
Palladium of drag, dear', Marc Fleming used to remark
bitterly.

Despite its austerity the dressing room was almost a hal-
lowed place. Rex had played the Cap so often it was like a
second home to him. Other artistes who appeared there
were very much aware that it was 'his' domain. In the
corner of the room were a couple of tea chests containing Mrs S's costumes most of which had been bought in
Camden jumble sales. A moth eaten fur, a faded 1950's
print frock, a pair of tiny red brogues — Mrs S's 'sensible'
shoes. There was a choice of wigs, grey, brown, even a blue
rinse. Mrs S — all in a wooden tea chest.

A macabre footnote to The Black Cap occurred in 1981
when gay serial killer Dennis Nilsen met Carl Stotter, a
drag act who performed in the pub as Khera Le Fox. Nilsen
took Stotter home to his flat in Cranley Gardens, Muswell
Hill. After passing out from strangulation, Stotter came to
while Nilsen was trying to drown him in a bath of water
and fortunately managed to fight him off.

Two of Rex's greatest admirers were the comedy actor
Jonathan Cecil and his wife, musical comedy star Anna
Sharkey. 'We were Shufflewick groupies,' said Jonathan.

'We often went to the Black Cap and various other strange venues all over London just to see him. One day I invited him back to our house in Chiswick for lunch. I was surprised that he accepted because he was rather shy. After a few glasses of wine he relaxed. I told him he would make a marvellous Fool to someone's King Lear. He was amused but didn't think he could learn the lines. I've often thought that if I ever played the Fool I would base it on Mrs Shufflewick and Rex.'

Drag Pubs

During the seventies drag pubs produced some of the best live entertainment in London. Seasoned variety stars such as Billy Wells and George Williams could be seen at venues all over the capital and acts such as The Harlequeens, Alvis and O'Dell, Terry Gardener, Chris Shaw and Rogers and Starr made drag popular with both gay and straight audiences. There were huge gay discos as well such as Bang in Charing Cross Road and Subway in Leicester Square where patrons included fashion guru Molly Parkin plus legendary filmmaker Derek Jarman with dyed bright orange hair and often wearing a cloak from his film *Sebastiane.*

Rex played them all, discos included, but there was one date which every drag act will remember with horror — The Elephant and Castle pub at Vauxhall Bridge. When you played the Elephant you had reached the very bottom of showbusiness. There was nowhere lower to go. Filthy dirty, damp and smelly and with cracked windows which overlooked Vauxhall junction, the pub was haunted by deadbeats and drunken Irishmen. Whoever thought of staging drag shows there must have escaped from Broadmoor.

When the unfortunate drag act appeared (to no backing because no musician would play there) they were either met with a wall of silence or, worse still, various shouts of 'Piss off, you poof!' or 'Go on darling, give us a wank!' Nine times out of ten the act did not survive five minutes and was hurriedly paid off by the bar staff. A fiver was the going rate.

Rex only played the place once and that was before I was his manager. He staggered bravely through his act but ended with the words: 'Ladies and Gentlemen, I have played some of the finest variety theatres in the country but I can truthfully say that this is the worst fucking dump I have ever come across.' A beer bottle narrowly missed him.

I am happy to say that The Elephant and Castle is no more. It was demolished some time ago. Whoever did it deserves a medal.

The Toupee

Rex, in his fifties, was almost bald and wore a permanent, rather mangy, toupee. He rarely removed the piece, even going so far as to wear it on stage under Mrs S's wig. Watching him make-up and trying to keep the grotty toupee straight while sticking an elderly lady's wig on top was an experience.

He rang me one morning and told me that disaster had struck. He had lost the precious toupee after a drunken night on the tiles. Would I ring up comic George Williams (equally bald) and ask if he had a spare? George did and so the three of us arranged to meet in the front bar of the Cap.

George arrived with a discreet parcel containing the toupee and slipped it to Rex. Rex, who had no shame about anything, tore open the parcel and began trying on the hairpiece in full view of the entire pub. It was too big so he asked the barman for a pair of scissors and began to trim it. Snips of false hair littered the floor while pub regulars looked on aghast.

George raised his eyebrows. I looked at the ceiling. 'My dears, it fits,' said Rex triumphantly. 'You can buy me a drink, Pat.'

Mrs Shufflewick top of the bill in pantomime with fellow toupee wearer comedian George Williams

THE REGAL THEATRE
WEST STREET – BOSTON

Manager – R. Aspland Howden
Telephone 2921
Box Office open 10 a.m. to 8 p.m.

Opens 26 Dec. at 2.15

JACK DENMAN
presents

Mrs SHUFFLEWICK
Radio and T.V.'s Most Curious Character
in
THE ALL COMEDY PANTOMIME

Babes in the Wood
featuring
BILLY SHAW & THE SHOWSTOPPERS
The Tricia Stone Dancers and Corps de Ballet
ROBERT   MARRADAY
COLMAN   PRESTON
Singing Star of "Camelot"   Star of "Snow White"

with the Comedy Star of over 800 Broadcasts

GEORGE WILLIAMS
"I'M NOT WELL"
KAY and KIMBERLEY
THE JANICE SUTTON JUVENILES
MIKE SHAYNE

SEE OVERLEAF FOR BOOKING FORM
APPLICATION FOR SEATS AND FULL
DETAILS OF TIMES AND PRICES

When me and my old man were first married I
didn't know much about cooking, I admit that.
I had two lamb chops I was going to do for him
and I put them in the oven on a low gas and I
suddenly felt the urge. So I went down to the old
Cock and Comfort and I'm afraid I overdid it.
And of course when I got back he was stood there
with the oven door open — they were like two
burnt offerings. He did his nut. He said 'I'm not
having you cooking on that stove, I'm going out
tomorrow to buy you a griller.' I don't know what
he thinks I'm going to do with one of those blessed
great hairy things running round the house.

Private Life

Rex rarely talked about his private life but at the beginning of the seventies he admitted publicly that he was gay. He flirted outrageously backstage with men in the dressing room at the Black Cap and in 1973 he gave an interview with *Gay News* in which he talked about his life and career as well as commenting on the gay scene of the day. 'There's a lot of fellas who would dearly love to go with a chicken,' he said, 'but they won't in case the people next door find out. No one bothers about a fella picking up a woman and going off but if it's a young lad, oh, it's terrible.'

When questioned, however, on what he thought of radical organisations such as the Gay Liberation Front (GLF) he was hesitant to commit himself:

'GLF? Well, I think, if I may say so, it's the wrong thing to do. Because I don't think you'll get people to join if you do things like that. I might be wrong — I've only seen it once, that was outside the Black Cap. They were going to do an event at Kentish Town, and they came up outside the Black Cap with leaflets and all that. I think there must be a better way to do it.

You're bound to get a lot of people who aren't going to have anything to do with GLF at all, because they don't understand it, and they are the people who are going to run you into the ground. I mean if their job's going to depend on it, they're not going to scream the place down, are they?'

A minority of gay activists took offence at the whole concept of Mrs Shufflewick, deeming her an old fashioned stereotype, the pinnacle of what Barry Took — no fan of Mrs S — objected to in general about female impersonation — 'the point they make is that women are vulgar and obnoxious, stupid, dirty-minded, sexually aggressive or anti-social' (*The Listener* 27.01.83). Yet throughout the decade Rex remained one of the most popular performers for gay men and women in Britain. Even off-stage Mrs S was in demand. Rex was regularly asked to be a celebrity judge at Andrew Logan's *Alternative Miss World* pageants and on two occasions he was driven majestically, as Mrs S, on a giant float through the West End as part of the annual Gay Pride march.

The American activist, Larry Mitchell, asserted that 'there is more to be learned from wearing a dress for the day than there is from wearing a suit for life' and the UK's radical

GLF Street Theatre Group believed that to wear drag on the underground or to the shops was an 'empowering act of confrontation'. Ironically, Rex, who often arrived at a working engagement dressed as Mrs S, had been shopping in drag for years — long before gay activism was born.

Most of Rex's relationships with men — and occasionally women — had been short lived, one night stands or brief affairs which had happened while he was touring in variety. Mel Dunn, wife of Bernard Dunn, one of Rex's regular pianists, came to know Rex in the seventies and felt that he was uneasy with women. 'Although we were friends, I'm not sure that deep down he really liked women,' she said whilst Bob Monkhouse observed that 'Rex had none of his creation's self-assertion. He carried the burden of rejection, always getting dumped by men he should never have loved in the first place.' In 1969, however, he met David Buckley, a burly Lancashire labourer in his thirties. David was an alcoholic who, when sober, was charm personified but after a heavy drinking bout could be aggressive.

Apart from their fondness for alcohol, Rex and David actually had a lot in common. Both were loners, drifters who had moved from one place to another without ever settling. Neither enjoyed family ties or lasting relationships. Both had the same gritty sense of humour and both loved gambling on the horses.

David moved into Rex's rundown flat in Falkland Road, Kentish Town, in 1969 on a casual basis. The arrangement depended on what alcoholic or financial state either of them was in. If David was drunk he would often sleep rough, somewhere in the neighbourhood, and return two or three days later, a dishevelled wreck. He was frequently unemployed and relied on Rex for money but, to be fair, when he received state benefits he always shared them with Rex. Rex's nickname for David was 'Myra' — as in moors murderess Myra Hindley — and he would often ring me with the gleeful information, 'It's Myra's payday!'.

I don't suppose I ever really understood their relationship. David told me that Rex didn't want sex. Rex told me it was the other way round. Whatever happened, both of them slept in separate beds. I liked David but the two of them often fought furiously and it was a common sight to see one or the other sporting a black eye. When their arguments became so fierce, Rex would turn up at my house, often in the middle of the night, and demand refuge. 'I've left him for good,' he would say firmly, ransacking my cupboards for Guinness or Scotch. I never commented because I knew he would return to David the next day. They were wildly possessive about each other and in an odd way it could be argued that Rex's sturdy, if often stuporous, sense of himself (as a gay man, living with David) gave his Mrs Shufflewick act a depth and ironic honesty it might not otherwise have had.

I shared my home in London at the time with my friend the actor Richard Ruck who worked late in the evenings as a compère in a West End nightclub. Richard's bedroom adjoined the hallway and whenever Rex turned up to stay for a night I would give him a folding bed which fitted neatly into the hallway. He was not keen on the folding bed — he was apt to fall out of it when drunk — and it was not unusual for Richard to return home late from work and find his own bed occupied by a tiny huddled figure, recognisable only by the flat cap which peeped out over the covers. Richard was not amused.

Like Richard, I endured my share of Rex's nocturnal habits. One night Richard was already asleep in his own bed and Rex was adamant about not using the folding bed in the hall. 'I'll sleep with you, dear,' he said to me, giving a loud burp — he had just polished off a half bottle of Scotch — 'It'll be much easier.' My heart sank. Without removing his baggy suit or cap he climbed into bed with me and pulled up the covers. 'There, dear, that's not so bad, is it?'

He fell asleep almost instantly and then snored all night. It was the most uncomfortable night I have ever spent in my life, but in the annals of showbiz history I can truthfully say I once slept with Mrs Shufflewick.

The Icon

The work I got for Rex in the seventies and early eighties was probably the most varied of his career although it was not as profitable financially as his heydays in variety. But he had become a comic icon. 'You've been rediscovered,' I said to him one day. 'I know,' he replied drily, 'I've been rediscovered every six weeks of my life.'

He teamed up again with Dot Squires, this time for a two week season at the Victoria Palace with Roy Walker and Bernie Flint, appeared in music hall seasons at Greenwich and Stratford East and did a cameo in the Marty Feldman film *Every Home Should Have One*. Filmmaker Tony Palmer featured him, along with Mae West and Liberace, in his classic TV documentary about the history of popular music, *All You Need Is Love*, and he overcame his long distrust of northern audiences by appearing in clubs and cabaret venues in Blackpool and North Wales.

In 1980 he made his final recording, a cassette, *Mrs Shufflewick Live at the Havajah Club*. The female impersonator Alan Haynes, who ran the Soho club gave us the premises rent free for the day. Danny La Rue came along to the live recording and brought crates of champagne and a crowd of friends with him. Before recording side two, Rex asked me to get Danny to introduce him.

Alan Haynes, who ran the Havajah Club in Soho where Rex made the recording *Mrs Shufflewick live at the Havajah* in 1980, with Danny La Rue

Danny obliged and gave a touching speech, ending with the words, 'We all love her because she's our dear Shuff.' The audience warmly applauded, Mrs S appeared and promptly said, 'How did 'e get in? Touting for business, I suppose . . .'

Ups and Downs

Rex was not a manic depressive and neither did he suffer from the Pagliacci 'Laugh, clown, laugh' syndrome. But he did have his black moods, usually after a bout of whiskey drinking. In the seventies Johnny Dallas was starring in pantomime at Luton and he and the cast went to see Rex who was doing a one nighter at the Pan Club, Luton. 'On arrival Rex was charming and friendly and went off to change,' said Johnny. 'But when he came down thirty minutes later and I said 'are you OK?' he just turned on me and said 'who the fuck are you?' and swept off.'

He was often plagued with insecurity and shifts of mood. When I first got him the London Palladium date with Dorothy Squires he came to stay with me a couple of nights beforehand. I'd picked up a recording of *Dot at the Palladium* and we played it one evening. As Rex drank more and more and listened to the loud applause for Dot on the LP, he kept saying, 'I can't do it, I mean I can't go on the same bill with that kind of star. I'm just not in that league.' It was no good trying to convince him that he was just as talented as Squires, if not more so. But the next morning he was his impish self and began to wickedly mimic Squires singing Peggy Lee's classic *Is That All There Is?*

The other morning I was in my front room dusting my best coffee service which used to belong to the Baron Rothschild. I know that because he initials are still on the side of the cups. Suddenly there was a knock at the bell and there was this woman shaking a collecting box. She said 'The Battersea Dogs' Home.' I said, 'I didn't know the bleedin' thing had been away.' I wouldn't have given her anything because I'm not mad about dogs. I went into my local one night and I was stood there with my brandy and suddenly I looked down and there was this large Dalmation dog licking its parts. I didn't know what to do with meself; I wished the ground would open and swallow me up. Suddenly I looked round and there's this six foot Irishman and he said, 'I wish I could do that, missus.' So I said, 'Well, if you give it a biscuit, it might let you.'

Managing Rex would give anyone a headache. For every two dates that he performed brilliantly there was the one where he was so drunk that it was embarrassing for the audience and even worse for me. Pub and club managers never vented their spleen on Rex, they shouted at me. There was jealousy from other comedians. Ken Platt, a comic I knew well and admired, once told me to stop managing Rex. 'You'll do yourself no favours associating with him,' he said. There were also the lost opportunities. I tried to get him a role in the film *Wildcats of St Trinian's* — he would have been wonderful as a dipsy gym mistress — but the casting director for the film was less than impressed at the sight of a boozy, unshaven Rex. He was shortlisted to appear as a special guest on Michael Parkinson's top rating TV chat show but a preliminary meeting with a researcher turned to disaster when David turned up drunk and he and Rex started arguing.

But I loved managing him and there were endless compensations. The long conversations about variety in the dressing rooms, the surreal descriptions ('She was a lovely woman — the soul of epitome') and the laughs ('I hear

Dame May Whitty's playing the Vauxhall Tavern next week; they've got Flora Robson on the drums'), the shared drinks, watching him make-up and then seeing him go out on stage and tear an audience up. Few were as lucky as me to watch a great comic at work at such close quarters. More than that, we were friends. Good friends.

I've been under my doctor for six months, on and off. He's a big fella, Dr McKankie. He used to be a horse slaughterer only he changed his mind in mid air one Wednesday afternoon when he was messing about with a stallion and now he does it with people. I go down every Tuesday evening to see him. I go in the evenings because his hands are warmer. I was sitting in his insulting room and there's this woman sitting beside me and oh, she was in a state; quaking all over. I said, 'Whatever's the matter, dear, can't you keep still?' She said, 'No, it's the whiskey, it always gets me like this. ' So I said, 'you want him to give you something to stop you drinking it'. She said, 'no, I want him to give me something to stop spilling it'.

Rex was fifty-six in 1980 and I was twenty-five. He looked over seventy and his health was failing. Heavy smoking caused him to cough incessantly and thanks to alcohol he had lost his appetite. Sometimes he could go on a bender and disappear completely and then have to lie down at home in bed to recover for two days. 'I'm suffering from whiskey-itis' he would say ruefully. Occasionally I wouldn't hear from him for a week and then discover that he had gone to Southend on his own and stayed in a boarding house, perhaps to recapture childhood memories. Who knows? He never said.

By 1980 he and David had been evicted from their flat in Kentish Town and had found a furnished room in Mornington Terrace, Camden Town, where they lived in similar domestic chaos. David took odd labouring jobs and Rex had plenty of dates in his book. Although Rex loved working, by now he felt jaded with everyday life. Conservative by nature, he felt old fashioned and hated change. Modern films were too violent. Camden Town had changed. Many of his variety pals were dead. When the writer Michael Pointon asked him in 1980 whether he ever regretted submerging his own character into that of Mrs Shufflewick, he was nonchalant. 'If I got up on stage in a suit and did an act no one would recognise me, would they?' he said. 'They want to see this drunken old tart.'

I'm going to pop off now and I'll tell you why. I've left a large whiskey going cold and I had one knocked over in 1927 and I still wake up screaming about that . . .

Here's to Rex . . .

Ralph Reader once commented that Rex could have been as big a star as Tony Hancock or Peter Sellers if he had 'disciplined himself.' Bill Pertwee, who had worked with Rex at the Windmill, disagrees. 'I believe that some of the man's brilliance and unique talent might have disappeared into mediocrity if he had been disciplined,' he said. 'So many people had a warm affection for Shuff, not just for the character Mrs Shufflewick he portrayed on stage but also for Rex Jameson, the gentle alcoholic he became. The pleasure he brought to his audiences far outweighed any problems he might have brought to theatre managements.'

Looking back no one could ever have stopped Rex from drinking, least of all me. Mrs Shufflewick, Rex Jameson or just Shuff — they were all the same character. Booze equalled all three.

Conceived in variety, born on radio, graduated on television and maturing in live entertainment, Mrs Shufflewick was a rare creation. The end for the 'drunken old tart' and for Rex — Shuff, if you like — came unexpectedly on 5 March 1983. He had been working at the Black Cap at lunchtime and afterwards had returned to Mornington Terrace. I had booked him that night to top a variety bill at the Theatre Royal, Stratford East. At around four o'clock he left his flat to get a packet of cigarettes and stock up on Guinness from a local store off Camden High Street. Without warning he collapsed in the street and lost consciousness. A passer by phoned for an ambulance and he was rushed to the Royal Free Hospital where he was pronounced dead on arrival. The official cause of his death was that he had suffered a heart attack. He would have been 59 in June that year.

His funeral, like his life, was unconventional. I didn't expect that many people would attend, perhaps just a handful of friends, but on the day over 500 people gathered outside the chapel at Golders Green Crematorium. There were actors, drag queens, comedians, fans, and simply the curious. Flowers and wreaths were everywhere. Rex had made no will and therefore died intestate. The Entertainment Artistes Benevolent Fund paid for the funeral.

Television cameras crowded around Danny La Rue and Ernie Wise as they told their own Mrs S stories. Cameras flashed and celebrities signed autograph books for the starstruck. Comedian Dickie Henderson, in a sotto voce tone, turned to a friend and muttered wryly, 'If they dropped a bomb on this lot, there wouldn't be a poof left in England.'

The service was straight forward, simple but emotional. Bernard Dunn, one of Rex's favourite accompanists, led the congregation with the hymn *All Things Bright And Beautiful* and read from the book of Corinthians ('Though I speak with the tongues of men and angels . . .'). Lew Lane from the EABF gave a brief résumé of Rex's career. At the front of the chapel lay the tiny white coffin which somehow looked smaller than Rex did in real life. A single spray of freesia had been placed on the top by David and next to it I had put Rex's flat cap. As the coffin was ready for the committal, Bernard played Rex's signature tune, *My Old Man Said Follow The Van* and the entire congregation joined in loudly, some of them weeping. A brief silence was observed and then we all dispersed outside into the sunshine.

There is no grave or memorial stone to Rex. After he died a flurry of drag performers were quick to jump on to the comedy bandwagon, rip off the famous Mrs S routines and present them in the form of various 'tributes'. It was depressing. But as time went on a new, younger generation, most of whom had been nurtured on 'alternative' comedy, discovered Rex's unique brand of humour mainly through bootleg tapes and CD's taken from his three main recordings. BBC Radio shows were often asked to play Mrs Shufflewick and in the flourishing trend for books written about classic British comedy the name Rex Jameson began to feature regularly. I've often thought that if Rex were around today he would have been lionised by the likes of Matt Lucas, Peter Kay and other talented young comedians. Mrs Shufflewick hasn't dated.

I lost touch with David Buckley after Rex died but ten years later fate intervened in unexpected circumstances. I was living in a flat in St Martin's Lane in London and one day I found David sleeping rough in an alleyway nearby. He had been evicted from Rex's flat in Camden Town as soon as Rex had died. Outwardly cheerful, but desperately lonely without Rex, he was rootless again. I tried to help in various ways but he was a proud man and refused charity. However, on several occasions, we did enjoy a drink together.

One afternoon he came round to the flat clutching a large bottle of cider. On a shelf he spotted one of Rex's recordings. It was the LP made live at the Black Cap. 'Play that,' he said. 'I used to love that record.'

I put the LP on the turntable. Rex's gags came quick and fast. David started to laugh loudly and so did I. At the end of the recording he wiped away his tears — tears of laughter. 'Rex was so funny, wasn't he?' he said. 'Yes, he was,' I said. We both smiled and I cracked open another drink. Cheers, Rex.

A rare shot of Rex (left) out of drag — complete with cloth cap — pictured in 1979 with comedian Billy Wells

Mrs S — 'Weak willed and easily led' — pictured backstage at Battersea Town Hall 1978

ACKNOWLEDGEMENTS

I should like to thank the following for their help with this book: Peggy Bennett, Jonathan Cecil, Duggie Chapman, Johnny Dallas, Keith Evans, Peter Goodwright, Bryan Hooton, Roy Hudd OBE, Bernard Maeder, Mike Major, Eric Midwinter, Dennis Norden OBE, Chubby Oates, William Owen, Gerry Oxley, Bill Pertwee MBE, Jack Seaton, Jennie Sheppard, David Simpson Hugh Small and John Wade. I am particularly grateful to Michael Pointon and Richard Anthony Baker for their advice and encouragement.

BIBLIOGRAPHY

Baker, Richard Anthony — *British Music Hall* (Sutton Publishing 2006)

Baker, Roger — *Drag* (Cassell 1994)

Cottle, Gerry — *Confessions of a Showman* (Vision 2006)

Farson, Dan — *Marie Lloyd and the Music Hall* (Tom Stacey 1972)

Fisher, John — *Funny Way To Be A Hero* (Muller 1973)

Monkhouse, Bob — *Over The Limit* (Century 1998)

Nathan, David — *The Laughter Makers* (Peter Owen 1970)

Wall, Max — *The Fool on the Hill* (Quartet Books 1975)

RECORDINGS OF MRS SHUFFLEWICK

Look In At The Local (Ace of Clubs Label 1964), with Ida Barr and Kim Cordell. Recorded live at the Waterman's Arms.

The Amazing Mrs Shufflewick: Live at the New Black Cap (Decca 1973).

Mrs Shufflewick Live at the Havajah Club (Audio Arts cassette 1980)

Up Town At The Downtown (TVT Telstar video 1980) featuring Mrs Shufflewick, Lee Tracey and The Pure Corn Company. Studio recording with canned laughter.

There are plans for a compilation CD of Mrs Shufflewick recordings to be released in 2008.

Index of artistes

Other Third Age Press books
by Eric Midwinter

As one ^ door closes . . . The story of John Wade: Jobbing Conjuror

stage

As one stage door closes . . . is a study of the way the entertainment world has changed over the past 50 years by shifts in the social and economic fabric, as personally witnessed by John Wade, who, over that period, has successfully plied the ancient craft of magicianship in every possible show-business outlet. In the course of his personal journey, he crosses paths with a sparkling array of stars. This book contrives to look both in front of and behind the scenes – and then locates both in social context. From the dingy theatrical lodgings and dreary train journeys of the 1950s to the sumptuous environs of luxury liners and Hollywood glamour 40 years on, this show-business saga unrolls. **176 pages £12.50**

Novel Approaches: a guide to the popular classic novel

Oh for a good read and an un-putdownable book! Despite the lurid blandishments of television, there are still many of us who turn, quietly, pensively, to the novel in leisure moments. This short text is aimed at such people whose interest has been kindled sufficiently to permit some extra contemplation and study.

Novel Approaches takes 35 novels that have stood the test of time and embeds them in historical and literary commentary – a combination of social background giving scientific objectivity, and the author's artistic subjectivity.

180 pages £9.50

THIRD AGE PRESS

. . . an independent publishing company which recognizes that the period of life after full-time employment and family responsibility can be a time of fulfilment and continuing development . . . a time of regeneration

Third Age Press books are available by direct mail order from **Third Age Press, 6 Parkside Gardens London SW19 5EY** . . . or on order through book shops.

dnort@globalnet.co.uk   www.thirdagepress.co.uk

1 or 2 books (UK) postfree - please add £1 postage for each additional book. Please add 20% for other countries. UK Sterling cheques payable to *Third Age Press*.

 *. . is a series that focuses on the presentation of your unique life. These booklets seek to stimulate and guide your thoughts and words in what is acknowledged to be not only a process of value to future generations but also a personally beneficial exercise.*

A Voyage of Rediscovery: a guide to writing your life story
. . . is a 'sea chart' to guide your reminiscence & provide practical advice about the business of writing or recording your story.
36 pages   £4.50

Encore: a guide to planning a celebration of your life
An unusual and useful booklet that encourages you to think about the ways you would like to be remembered, hopefully in the distant future.   **20 pages   £2.00**

The Rhubarb People . . . Eric Midwinter's own witty and poignant story of growing up in Manchester in the 1930s. Also on tape including useful tips on writing or recording your story.
32 pages   £4.50
~ audio cassette   £5.00

OR all 3 booklets for only £10 including p & p

Also from Third Age Press . . .

On the Tip of Your Tongue: your memory in later life

by Dr H B Gibson . . . explores memory's history and examines what an 'ordinary' person can expect of their memory. He reveals the truth behind myths about memory and demonstrates how you can manage your large stock of memories and your life. Wittily illustrated by Rufus Segar. **160 pages £7.00**

A Little of What You Fancy Does You Good: your health in later life
by Dr H B Gibson

'Managing an older body is like running a very old car – as the years go by you get to know its tricks and how to get the best out of it, so that you may keep it running sweetly for years and years' . . . so says Dr H B Gibson in his sensible and practical book which respects your intelligence and, above all, appreciates the need to enjoy later life. It explains the whys, hows and wherefores of exercise, diet and sex ~ discusses 'You and your doctor' and deals with some of the pitfalls and disabilities of later life. Illustrated by Rufus Segar. **256 pages £7.00**

**Buy both the above books
for the special price of only £10.00**

An exciting new book from **Third Age Press** . . . mature
women writing on a wide range of thought provoking subjects

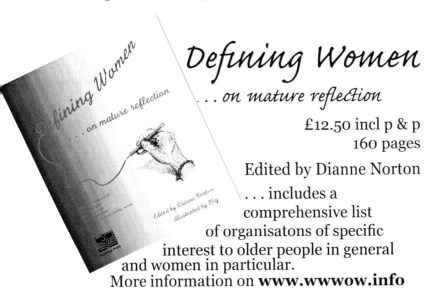

Defining Women

. . . on mature reflection

£12.50 incl p & p
160 pages

Edited by Dianne Norton

. . . includes a
comprehensive list
of organisatons of specific
interest to older people in general
and women in particular.
More information on **www.wwwow.info**

*The 'extraordinary ordinary women' invited to contribute
to this anthology rose magnificently to the occasion, delving
deep into their personal experiences and laying bare their
innermost feelings as they met a variety of challenges. The
book includes a report of research into the film industry
- why aren't older actresses chosen more often to play
appropriate parts and why are younger models used to
advertise cosmetics and other items specifically aimed at
the 60- plus market? Marriage is put under the spotlight
and so is grandmothering. The quality of writing is superb.
Mig's cartoons are a delight.* Gwen Parrish, U3A News

*Defining Women is a 'must have' book . . . stimulating thought,
laughter and discussion and anyone will be sure to find many
items of interest in it. Every page commands your attention.
I will finish by saying that this book is a real gem. Buy it and
cherish it.* July Newsletter - www.hagsharlotsheroines.com

RAVES & REVIEWS

Unforgettable. This biography with all the laughter and desperation is a must for the bookshelf of every entertainment afficianado. WYN CALVIN

A great read. A book that is written eloquently and touchingly. ROBERT ELMS

I read this book to find out more about the iconic Mrs Shufflewick, but I discovered the amazingly talented Rex Jameson. It's been a delightful journey. Pour a stiff one and read this book. MIKE WILKINS, *Gay Times*

An affectionate memoir of one of the 20th century's great drag performers. PETER BURTON, *3Sixty Magazine*

A truly wonderful book. BARRY CRYER

I loved it! VICTOR SPINETTI

Patrick Newley has written a book which is almost as sad as it is funny and is immensely readable. JOHN WADE, *Encore Magazine*

Newley interweaves the text with extracts from Shuff's scripts which are so skillfully written that one can imagine how Jameson played them and get a real flavour of what meeting Mrs Shufflewick was really like. For those who saw Mrs S live, this is a wonderful reminder of that talent and a fitting tribute clearly written with great affection. TOM HOWARD, *Rogues and Vagabonds*

A book that is both very funny and very sad. Patrick Newley is a superb anecdotalist, who does not fail us here. RICHARD ANTHONY BAKER, *The Stage*